50 Years of Hunting and Fishing

The Mis-Adventures of a Guy Who Couldn't Quit!

PART I

Ben D. Mahaffey

Writers Club Press
San Jose New York Lincoln Shanghai

50 Years of Hunting and Fishing
The Mis-Adventures of a Guy Who Couldn't Quit!

All Rights Reserved © 2000 by Ben D. Mahaffey

No part of this book may be reproduced or transmitted in any form or by any means, graphic, electronic, or mechanical, including photocopying, recording, taping, or by any information storage or retrieval system, without the permission in writing from the publisher.

Published by Writers Club Press
an imprint of iUniverse.com, Inc.

For information address:
iUniverse.com, Inc.
620 North 48th Street
Suite 201
Lincoln, NE 68504-3467
www.iuniverse.com

ISBN: 0-595-00428-8

Printed in the United States of America

Contents

Introduction v
A Tribute vii
Redneck Philosophy 1
Early Memories of Hunting and Fishing 9
A Lifetime of Experiences 13
Alaska Adventures 17
Is the Gun Loaded? 23
Cabela's New Rod Design 39
Caribou Have White Feet 53
The Honeymoon Hunt 61
Second Chance 67
Over Confidence 73
A Missed Geography Lesson 77
The Dancing Buck 83
Real Guides Don't Smoke 89
Hunting the Wind River Range 99
Cow Elk Have Long Necks 101
Machine-Gun Kelly 107
The Bugling Bulls 111
The Unwanted Companion 115

The Wild Bull Ride 119
The Great Bear Robbery 127
The Addict 131
The Missing Glove 143
The Duckery 153
The Floppy-Eared Buck 159
Give Me a .30-06 Dog 165
Half-Price Sale 177
The Idaho Scam 191
The Realtor 203
Shared Shelter 209
The Gun Rest 217
The Delta Force 223
Guilty as Charged 233
Re-Wind and Fast-Forward 237
About the Author 241

Introduction

I recently finished reading two books by Theodore Roosevelt on his hunting experiences. I knew that he was an avid hunter and conservationist but I didn't know that he wrote so extensively on hunting. There are other volumes of his on hunting that I will be reading soon. He also wrote several award winning volumes on *The Winning of the West*. These volumes were entertaining and motivating.

As a result of reading his experiences, I thought that I would record some of my hunting and fishing experiences. These true stories were originally written as an appendix to an already completed condensed version of my autobiography. However, as I continued to record them, they took on a life of their own and an appendix became a book.

Please note: the names used in some of the stories have been changed to protect the innocent and to save embarrassment to the guilty. However, in some accounts, those named are the actual people. Each account is true, with some embellishment here and there, to add interest for the reader. The stories are not always in chronological order.

I realize that my experiences were nothing compared to Teddy's! But there didn't appear to be any humor in his experiences; at least he didn't show any in his writing. My stories, though not about Africa, have taken place in 11 lower states and Alaska. Some were humorous in places, others were more catastrophic in nature. I learned a long time ago that many trips have been saved and enjoyed by viewing them humorously. Unfortunately, this often has to be done in retrospect and not at the time!

A Tribute

The purpose of life becomes more focused when viewed from the perspective of age. It is becoming increasingly obvious to me that when life's distractions are cast aside, there is nothing more valuable than family and friends.

An appendix to an autobiography has become a book, much the result of my wife Barbara's encouragement. Indeed, she has supported me for almost a half century. I love her dearly and we are family and friends. Although she has never understood my passion for the outdoors and hunting and fishing, she has been supportive. I recall, many years ago when she said: "Ben, there is a lot of our monthly budget disappearing and I think it is being spent on your expensive habits." I responded: "Hunting and fishing are cheaper than being under a psychiatrist's care." She then told me: "It may be cheaper, but it's not working."

I introduced my oldest son, Mark, to fishing when he was three years old. I stopped at one of those pay-as-you-fish ponds in Fort Collins, Colorado. He caught three and wanted more, but I was out of money. He is addicted to fishing, builds rods, ties flies and must have caught thousands of fish by now. Mark, is it too late for one more hunt or another trip down the Kanectoc River?

My second Son, Clark is a modern "Techie." But he loves to fish and hunt. His priorities are sometimes confused and he lets work and other responsibilities get in his way of outdoor pursuits. And sometimes he still uses those "I-Gottem Shells." (A hunter who uses an "I-Gottem Shell," has an uncontrollable urge to yell out "I-Gottem" when any bird falls in the general area).

My youngest Son, Scott, is the "runt of the litter," but we are friends and hunters. Little did I realize, when I modestly introduced him to whitetail deer hunting that he would become so dedicated! He has also been known to carry some of those "I-Gottem Shells" in his pocket. Keep hunting, Scott and you will get a buck as large as the one I shot that hangs in your office.

To all those with whom I have shared many experiences, I say thank you. To: Russell Madsen, Terry Beaver, Clark Hatch, Ed Souders, Robert Ruude, Treavor Gott and the few others...Is there still time for one more trip?

Some companions have disappeared over time, the rest have long since died and gone to that Limited Entry Celestial Hunting and Fishing Area. I hope that some of you have sat on a ridge with the hopes of getting a shot at that lion before it lies down with the lamb.

Thanks to Dorothy Proud, my second mother-in-law, who was always telling me to write a book. But she never gave me a subject. I am sorry that she is not around to read it.

I am not sure what it is like up "there." But I hope *all hunters and fishermen* are enjoying the following conditions:

No need for snow chains
The creeks are never deeper than your boots
Open season all year
No game and fish wardens
The fish always bite
Birds always flush in range
Your wife is excited when you return
Outfitters never lie

BEN D. MAHAFFEY
Vernal, Utah

Redneck Philosophy

Hunting and fishing are common recreational pursuits, especially in the west. They were more common in the east before the extensive settlement that now exists. Hunting and fishing activities are also more common for men than women, although some women do hunt and fish, but few in comparison to men. Scott, (my youngest son) is teaching his oldest daughter Kiane to hunt, although her long term interest is unknown at this time. Stereotypical activities are slow in changing, although it appears that these sports would be more attractive to males. One reason for this is the difficult and often dangerous environments where these activities take place.

Another interesting phenomenon is that most who hunt and fish begin when youngsters. Few adults learn to hunt and fish. This is not true for other sports, i.e., golf, hiking, etc. However, at one time, I taught an older male friend to trap shoot and then to hunt birds. He became an avid hunter! It is *usually* a father figure who introduces youngsters to the sport.

Most hunters and fishermen begin as youngsters. Jim Beaver and Mark Mahaffey, Nebraska, 1971.

The other day, I was on the Internet negotiating with a guide for a possible deer hunt out of Buffalo, Wyoming. My wife, Barbara, learning of this said: "Haven't you had enough hunting, after a lifetime of it? Haven't you killed enough animals?" Good heavens! After a lifetime of me explaining to her that hunting is more than killing, she should ask these questions!

I tried to think of an example that would explain a life time of enjoying one activity. I thought of sex, but quickly changed my mind, fearing what she would say. I changed the subject to books. "Barbara, just because you have read scores of books, does that mean you are not interested in reading another one with an intriguing cover?" She didn't answer me, she just went into another room and picked up a book.

The socialization process, while hunting and fishing, is an interesting phenomenon. It is not unlike golf, photography, gardening and other recreational pursuits, in that the experience comprises many activities combined into one title. A good hunting or fishing trip takes planning, scheduling, plotting, buying, packing, meetings, phone calls, budgeting (I often call this rat-holing money from the wife), etc. And all of this is *before* the actual hunting trip. Each experience is different but often includes driving, camping, cooking, tracking, hiking and freezing. The killing is a small part of the whole experience. I have often found that planning the trip was as enjoyable as the trip itself.

With some hunters and fishermen, especially if they are related, i.e., fathers, sons, brothers, uncles, etc., hunting and fishing experiences become a permanent part of the social and psychological bonding between and among them. Those feelings, although almost never mentioned, and often misunderstood, are real! Those memories are *usually favorable*. However, some experiences are negative and result in some individuals abandoning those types of recreational activities. Hunting and fishing seems to bring out the best and worst behavior in individuals. Indeed, character traits can be studied with great accuracy in these situations.

Proponents of organized recreational sports like football and basketball advocate those activities to build character, physical prowess, teamwork, etc. But in my opinion, hunting and fishing can do all of the above and more. In addition to the fundamental advantages, most hunters and fishermen can learn about ecology, wildlife management, law enforcement, sociology, psychology and human relations! Few will gain that knowledge under those names, but none-the-less, the learning often takes place.

I have three sons, Mark, Clark and Scott. We have all had these experiences, together and in different family combinations. I don't know how these experiences have helped mold their characters, but they are all good men and hopefully, our love and association will continue to develop. I am also optimistic that they will pass down the family guns and other equipment that has been used for decades...With an opportunity for the grandsons and *granddaughters* to use them many times with *their fathers.*

The philosophy of spending money for hunting and fishing is not unlike spending money for other recreational activities. Most of us really don't want to know what anything has cost us. We might want to know what it is *going* to cost us so that we can extort the money from our wives, but don't remind us when the money is gone. All of us spend a lot more money that we realize and it would shock us if we computed it!

The cost of hunting and fishing licenses has really increased, far more than the average inflation rate during the past fifty years. I suspect that some state G&F economists would disagree. They would throw in all of the eco-babble of constant dollars, using graphs, pie charts, curves, break points, etc. If that wouldn't work then they would tell about increased service, research and development programs and other excuses for what has become a state and national problem: the burgeoning, restrictive and corrupt bureaucracies.

An antelope permit could be purchased for $5, in Wyoming, in the 1950's.

In the early 1950's I could buy a deer, elk and antelope permit for $5 each. The deer and elk permits also included bear, birds and fish. As a non-resident, I just mailed a check for $295, for only a deer permit. State G&F Departments are revenue generating agencies, as much, or more than natural resource managing agencies. Some states will only sell out-of-state-permits for deer and elk together. Idaho and Montana now charge around $800 for the combination license. Idaho is so efficient that you can call an 800 number, order your license and do all of the application on the phone. They charge a $25 fee for this service, in addition to the base price.

This past season, Utah sold 15,300 "bucks only" licenses for the northeast corner of the state. I doubt there are that many bucks in Utah and the west half of Colorado. Wyoming is so greedy that they have a special "pool" for out-of-state applicants. If you submit an additional $100, you have a "better chance" of drawing a permit.

Most of us don't have much sympathy or understanding for what other types of recreationists spend. As an example, I cannot understand what manner of man would pay $300 for green fees to play one game of golf at Pebble Beach Golf Course, in addition to all of the ancillary expenses. I also do not understand why a golfer says that exercise is the main reason for golfing and then uses a golf cart.

Golfers ask me how I can justify two four-wheelers. That's simple. I need one for me and for a friend when we hunt…a couple of times a year, more often, when possible. But I also need a boat to fish the local lakes; a pickup to pull the boat; and a camper or travel trailer to live in while fishing or hunting. It appears to me, however, that hunters and fishermen probably get more enjoyment for their money spent for these pursuits than most other outdoor recreationists. You can't eat a golf ball! In all fairness, I have harvested some game animals that I could not eat.

I had a friend review the draft of this book. He was very concerned as he commented: "If you publish this book, it will be a rallying cry for all of the environmentalist wackos and anti-hunters. It will do great harm to hunters across the country." I thought about his comments. I guess I could use the policitically correct words and phrases: "harvest," "reduction in numbers," "annual increment," etc., but an animal is killed, and death is a part of life for animals and people. Nature is cruel and so are *some* people. I have never met a hunter or fisherman who *intended* to be cruel.

Hunting and fishing with 4-wheelers is challenging for all who care to use the new machines, Utah, 1998.

Early Memories of Hunting and Fishing

My first recollection of hunting, of any kind, was when I was about five years old. We were living in a shanty, in an oil town called Bairoil, Wyoming. This was about 1938. Dave Mahaffey (stepfather) and others poached deer in the nearby hills for meat. I recall going out late one night to meet the men who had hidden the deer.

Later, we moved to Casper, Wyoming. Until this time, we moved around Wyoming and nearby states. Dave was working in the "oil patch." When I was about ten or eleven years old, I began to walk with Dave while hunting. I used to go with him occasionally while fishing but not often.

Antelope hunting is easy, usually performed from a vehicle with little walking or stalking. The shooting is more difficult because of the distance but the physical demands are not near as difficult as deer or elk hunting.

In the late 1930's and early 1940's, deer hunting was closed over most of the state. During WWII, few men were around to hunt but the season was opened. There will probably never be the quality of hunting as there was at that time. I was a kid and this was when I walked and hunted with Dave and began what has been a lifetime activity. We used to hunt south of Casper about 50 miles in some rugged areas that abounded with deer since the season had been closed for so long.

I never had any boots. Dave had boots. I had to hunt in low cut shoes and often they didn't fit well. If I ever complained Dave would threaten to leave me home. So I learned to suffer in silence for the sake of the hunt. I can remember some gigantic blisters! I never asked for boots and Dave appeared to be insensitive to my needs. However, when I grew older I made sure I had adequate hunting equipment, and that *my boys* would not be neglected.

Fourteen was the minimum age to hunt. I never got to try to shoot before that time. I often asked Dave to help me, but beyond having me go along, I had very little training from him other than watching. I didn't have a gun. Dave had purchased a .270 Winchester in the late 1930's and used that gun until he quit hunting, fifty years later. He thought that the .270 was the most superior of any gun!

Until that time he used an 8mm Lebel. This was a WWI French Army rifle. As I recall, it held two in the magazine and one in the barrel. He had customized it. He cut down the barrel and the stock. It recoiled so badly that he put buckshot in the butt to help hold it down. He loaned this gun to me. But, as I recall, he never taught me how to shoot it. I just picked it up and started hunting.

I used it one season. I was out hunting in the same general area with Dave, but hunting by myself. I was walking high on a ridge. I looked down below and there were four big bucks walking below me. I sat down and fired three times at them…missing each time. Each time I shot, the recoil of the gun caused the stock to come up and hit me in the mouth! My mouth looked as if I had been in a fist fight!

Later in the day, I came up on another huge buck laying down below me. The bullet hit right between his legs; I had missed again. I didn't do very well with iron sights! Thus ended the season. I vowed I would never use that gun again…and I didn't. I was working at the newspaper at the time and it was located next door to the Western Auto Hardware Store. I went in and said I wanted to buy a .30-06. (I had checked around and that caliber seemed the most popular). The clerk said "you and everyone else in Casper." The war was just over and there were no guns available. He told me he would "put me on the list." A few months later the gun came in He called me and I bought my first gun. I put a Weaver 3.3 scope on it and I never had any serious problems missing again.

Just before I graduated from high school, I went on an elk hunting trip with Dave and others. We used horses, which I hate. I don't mind having a horse to use for packing but I have since refused to hunt from a horse. Those experiences introduced me to deer and elk hunting. Although, I never killed any deer or elk before I went into the military, I was "hooked" and was anxious to go again as my military service came to an end.

My first antelope hunt was a little different than my first deer and elk hunt. I was hunting north of Casper by the river where all of the hotels and motels are now located. They were sand hills in those days and a safe haven for antelope. I had my new rifle. I hit my first antelope but it was a gut shot and Dave was very unhappy. He berated me for my poor shooting. But, although it was a poor shot, I did get the antelope. Since that time, I have an aversion for gut shots, although they occasionally happen. The animal is usually lost, especially a deer or elk. Antelope are easier to follow, if gut shot. Most of the animals that I have killed over a 50 year period have been well shot and very few animals have been lost!

I was introduced to pheasant hunting in my teens. There were other birds to hunt…ducks, geese and sage chickens but I didn't hunt them much before returning from the military. But we often hunted pheasants. We hunted around Riverton and, occasionally, around Kaycee. Most people did not know that pheasants existed up there but it was great hunting for a few years along the valleys, in the grain fields and even in the sage brush draws.

Dave had been shooting a Winchester Model 97, 12 gauge pump. At about the time I started hunting, he bought a Winchester Model 12. This was the premium gun of the time. He let me use the Model 97. I shot it until it blew up in my face one day.

I recall shooting my first pheasant, using the Model 97. We were hunting near Kaycee along some fence rows. I had been out other times but had never touched a feather! But remember, no training or practice. I just picked up the gun and started. It was a difficult day. The birds were wild and most were hens, which we did not shoot. The wind was also blowing, as it always does, in Wyoming.

I was standing below a fence line with heavy cover. I looked south and it appeared a bird was flying down the fence!. I waited and waited and sure enough, as it grew closer, it was a large rooster! It was a long shot and I didn't have any idea how much to lead it but I threw up that old Model 97, pulled up about ten feet ahead and let it go! Down came the rooster, with probably one pellet in the head. My first pheasant! I looked to see where Dave was, sighted him and ran to show it to him. He just looked at it, said nothing and continued walking down the fence.

I didn't fish the creeks much during those early years. I did go with the family when we went together. We went up to the Middle Fork of the Powder River and hiked down some of the canyons fishing. I never did well in those conditions. Kids have a tough time fishing in small creeks.

However, about this time, Dave bought a boat and called it the "Nita Ann" after my adopted sister Juanita. We used to fish Pathfinder Reservoir. Fishing was great in those days. There were no developments on the reservoir. No ramps, camping grounds, etc. It was very unusual to see another boat on the reservoir. The boat was launched in the mud or sand or whatever conditions. The fish were Rainbows, Cutthroats and German Browns. The fish averaged 2 pounds but often were much larger.

Those experiences were about the only ones that I had with Dave. After I returned from the military and married, I usually hunted and fished with other people. I had a difficult time with Dave's behavior. He was a poor sport, prone to losing his temper and generally unpleasant to be around. There is no other way that I can explain my feelings toward him. However, I do appreciate him introducing me to those outdoor recreation sports. I guess that I could say I enjoyed and learned *from him, in spite of him.*

A Lifetime of Experiences

I served In the Navy from 1950-1953 and so didn't get to hunt or fish during those years. While in Japan, in 1952, I went to the PX and found that they sold guns. I purchased a Winchester Model 25, 12 gauge shotgun which I brought home with me. I paid $55 for it! It was a cheaper version of the great Winchester Model 12. It was a solid frame, where the Model 12 could be broken down. A great gun. I killed a lot of birds with that gun.

I returned to Casper in October of 1953. I began my apprenticeship at the newspaper at that time and renewed old acquaintances. I went deer hunting with an old friend, Bob Knoble. We went out southwest of Casper. We went out to camp but left after dark. We were in an old pickup and hit a deer going out. We rolled right over it. I told Bob that he could stop and tag that one! He didn't think my suggestion was humorous. Later Bob got a large four pointer and I shot my first deer...a small three pointer.

In the eastern United States all points or tines or anything that might be considered a point on the antlers is counted, but in the west, at that time, only one side was counted. Now there is a different method to describe the points 4 x 4 or 5 x 5. However, there may be some exceptions around the country.

Hunting and fishing licenses have really changed through the years. I have a complete collection for the past half century. The style of paper, wording, requirements, etc. have evolved. In some states you could enlist in the military easier than get a hunting license. This illustrates social changes and new technology, as well as new products. Recently, I purchased a fishing license and tags in Texas. They were burped out of a machine and looked exactly like a grocery list. This is vastly different than some of older licenses that were on water-proof paper and had a certified look. You could show those with pride to a fish cop. It's just not the same when you pull out a grocery list.

I have hunted and fished for over 50 years. It is not the intent of this book to detail all experiences. However, I have hunted and/or fished in the following states:

Alaska	Montana
Arizona	Nebraska
California	Texas
Colorado	Utah
Idaho	Wyoming
Kansas	

I have killed the following game:

Antelope	Ducks (several species)
Whitetail Deer	Dove (two species)
Mule Deer	Geese (several species)
Elk	Sage Chicken
Caribou	Chuckar
Bobcat	Pheasants (several species)
Rabbit	Turkey
Grouse	

I have caught the following species of fish:

Rainbow	Halibut
Cutthroat	Redfish
German Brown	Speckled Sea Trout
Dollie Varden	Rock Fish (several species)
Grayling	Walleye

Salmon   Pike
Chinook   Lake Trout
Chum   Barricuda
Sockeye
Coho
Pink

I have had a few animals mounted and a few fish. However, I have hundreds of photos, some which have been used to illustrate this book. I have a large display of photos and animals in our office at Bellman Propane Inc., Randolph, Kansas.

Most of the animals that I have killed have been males. Often, only males can be taken but even when there is a choice, I have almost never shot females. This is also true of birds, when possible. Antler or horn size becomes the motivating and challenging factor for most big game species. However, at times, I have hunted for meat, in addition to the challenge. In these cases, females have been taken.

Alaska Adventures

In 1984 I made the first of many trips to Alaska. Two were on business but all of the others but one was for fishing. One trip was a combination caribou-salmon fishing adventure.

The first trip I took my youngest son, Scott. We spent two wonderful weeks touring Alaska with two fishing expeditions. I didn't know anyone who had been there to help guide me so we just flew up and I began to become generally acquainted with the state. We drove all of the major oil highways (not many). We drove from Anchorage up to Dinali National Park on to Fairbanks and then down the Alaska Pipeline through all of that country, by Valdez and back to Anchorage. We chartered a plane and flew *around* Mount Dinali (it is so high small planes cannot fly *over it*).

Mark and Clark visiting an inland glacier site, Alaska, 1986.

We took the railroad to Whittier, the secret port developed during WWII. We toured the Kenai Peninsula and fished for Halibut off Homer. Then we flew over to Lake Iliamna and fished the Newhalen River for Sockeye Salmon. We stopped in Soldotna and met John Mahaffey and his family. He is my Step Sister Nita's brother. (I will not try to explain those family ties).

We went on a chartered ship to visit the tidewater glaciers and watched as sections broke off (calving) in front of us! We also drove to see the land glaciers and noted how they had retreated during the past decades.

The fishing expeditions were secondary to the general touring. We had fun catching Sockeye and Halibut but those trips paled in compaison to others that I have made specifically for fishing. Alaska fishing and hunting can be incredible. However, like other places, guides and outfitters are notoriously dishonest and I had to learn the good ones by trial and error.

I took my oldest son Mark twice to Alaska fishing. One year we floated the Kanectoc River, a large, relatively unknown river from its beginning to the sea. We had an incredible trip, very exhausting but fun. Did we catch fish! We caught Grayling, Dolly Varden, Rainbow, Chum and Silver

Salmon. Our outfitter was new and very incompetent, but we survived and prevailed. I was swept off the raft twice but managed to get out of the river!

Refuges offer great opportunities for viewing wildlife, Alaska, 1985.

Fishing in Alaska, if you know where to go, is so incredibly successful that I have a hard time believing it, even while I am there fishing! Of course, almost all of the fish are returned. Then when ready to depart, fish are kept, and prepared to return. I have brought back hundreds of pounds of fish of all kinds!

There are five species of Salmon and I have been privileged to catch all of them at different times. However, they are not running at the same time in the same rivers. So, to catch all of them takes planning and more than one trip. The Chinook or King Salmon is the greatest of all! I have caught a lot of them, the largest being 42 pounds in the Kanectoc River.

The Silver is next for sport and then the Chum. The Sockeye and the Pink are very poor sport fish but good to eat! The Silver is the best for wet flies. However, King can be caught on wet flies. I doubt that any salmon can be caught on dry flies. I get excited just sitting here and writing about them! I would really enjoy going fishing in Alaska one more time. But I have lost most of my contacts; it is very expensive and I don't have anyone interested in going with me. However, I went by myself on many of the trips.

Alaska offers outstanding fishing. Scott, left, holds a 9-pound Sockeye Salmon, 1984. Clark, right, holds a 12-pound Silver Salmon, 1986.

On one trip I took both Mark and Clark and we had a great time. This trip was for Silvers and we caught lots of them! Then one time Clark was assigned to the National Guard in Anchorage for a couple of weeks. I met him there and we visited. He then went fishing on the Kenai with some of his friends.

I spent one week by myself on a houseboat down on the Panhandle in southern Alaska. This was for Pinks and various species of ocean fish, primarily Halibut. We caught quite a few. The largest I caught was a 60 pounder. They are interesting fish. Oh, I could go on! *Alaska is a feeling as well as a place.* It is difficult to describe it. If I were young, I would consider moving up there. I tried one time but conditions were not right and I had to abandon the idea. One thought…fishing and hunting must be done in the bush. Often, if access can be made by vehicle, it might not be any better than places in lower states. However, five minutes by air and everything changes!

Is the Gun Loaded?

The title of this story might indicate that it is about hunting, but this is a fishing experience. I went to Alaska many times during the 1980's and mid 1990's. I have fished over much of Alaska. There are many different places and ways to fish: trolling salt water, drifting salt water; trolling fresh water, drifting fresh water, using canoes, wading, etc. My favorite type of fishing is wading in the creeks and rivers. A special place to fish is at tidewater, where the salt and fresh water merge; a great place for salmon and other species. I have caught four different species in one hole at tidewater!

My oldest son Mark and I tried a different type of fishing in August, 1985, in Alaska. Mark was in the Navy and he and I corresponded for some time in planning this trip. The year before I had met some guides in the Western part of Alaska who recommended an outfitter who was going to take some parties down the Kanectoc River on a raft. It was about a hundred miles and would take about a week.

During the winter of 1984 I corresponded with the guide. It soon became evident that this would be his first experience at guiding. I was immediately skeptical and was about to abort...when he asked me to give him a chance. Every guide had to have a first experience with his first clients. Being the softy that I am, I yielded to his appeal, in spite of my better judgement.

I was living in Manhattan, Kansas at the time. Mark came home and we flew to Anchorage, Alaska. Anchorage is the hub for all air traffic.

From there we caught a small scheduled airline to Dillingham, a small native village in southwest Alaska. There we met our guide, whose name was Rene Limmeres (his name is a permanent part of my memory hard drive for experiences that I will describe). He had a new raft that had never been put into the water. His other equipment was minimal, and what would prove later, to my discomfort, inadequate!

We chartered a Beaver float plane at Dillingham, one of the old workhorses that have been around for so long. This was my first of many experiences with float planes. I was amazed at how large the floats were. I looked at their size and wondered how a plane would ever get off the water! They roar, vibrate, shake and finally lift off slowly and even slower when heavily loaded as we were. Our plans were to land on the lake where the Kanectoc River originated. The name of the lake was, as I recall, Kagati Lake. It was about ten acres. The river, at this beginning point, was about 20 feet wide. At the mouth of the Pacific, where we finished our trip, it appeared to be almost as big as the Missouri! There are so many rivers, streams and creeks in Alaska, that even a river of this size is relatively unknown to outsiders and most of the residents.

As we slowly gained altitude after leaving Dillingham, I was amazed to note the absence of any sign of man. This became of great interest to me. We flew for 45 minutes and during that whole time I never saw a road, a building or anything to even indicate that man had ever been in the area! This was a pleasant comparison to other debris-strewn sections of Alaska.

Our heavily loaded float plane touched down on the small lake without incident. The pilot taxied us to the mouth of the river and pulled up to a sand bar. This float plane had wheels on the bottom and he revved up the engine and pulled right on the sand bar. In a few minutes we had all of the gear unloaded and arranged on the sand bar. The plane taxied off the sand bar, turned north and roared away. I had a strange feeling as it disappeared into the clouds. In those days we had no cell phones, pagers or the neat new conveniences. I might have felt more comfortable if we even had a carrier pigeon.

I looked at the mouth of the river…crystal clear water, about a foot deep as it began tumbling toward the Pacific Ocean. While Rene looked for the pump to inflate the raft, Mark and I got our ultra light gear out. We had a selection of small lures that we used for trout in the lower states. About a hundred yards below the mouth of the river was a series of deep holes. Mark threw in his lure first. Wham, and the fight was on as an Arctic Grayling battled and moved into the rapids. Mark landed it and we looked at the first Grayling and the first fish caught on this trip. There didn't appear to be any other type of fish in those holes. I looked at the lake and wondered if there were any Pike there but we did not take time to find out. Pike are located in some lakes of Alaska. Pike is the only major species of fish that I have not caught in Alaska. We caught several more Grayling as Rene prepared our raft for travel. He finally found the pump. I was a little nervous after he told me that he had never inflated the raft before!

The raft was 20 feet long with a central compartment with a frame and oar locks. By the time we put in all of our camping gear, food and personal equipment, it was full, with a small space for Mark and me to ride. Rene would row and guide and Mark and I would rotate from riding in the front or rear. I was usually in the rear since it was easier to use our spinners from that location. However, riding in the rear, made it difficult to see any of the obstacles that might appear in the river.

We were on the river and moving by 2:00 p.m. The terrain was rough and broken into canyons with low shrubs and trees, some alders and low brush. It was not very high in elevation, perhaps 2000 feet. This lower elevation was one reason the river was great for rafting and fishing. As we traveled, small creeks and streams constantly ran into it from other small watersheds. From 20 miles down, clear to the coast, the area was basically flood plain. The scenery was boring and un-noteworthy. However, the water and the fishing was spectacular. Few animals were seen. However, bald eagles and waterfowl were quite common.

Since this was the first week in August, the day was bright and beautiful, with high fluffy clouds. But little did we realize that this was the rainy season in that part of Alaska. We caught more Grayling and by evening, we began to catch Dolly Varden, one of my favorite Alaska fish. It began to appear that different species of fish inhabited the river at different locations. The Dolly Varden was a beautiful fish and reminded me of the Brook Trout of the Rocky Mountains, but much larger. They averaged, perhaps 2 pounds, with some reaching 3 pounds in certain locations. They fight with vigor and respond very well to wet and often dry flies. Rene found a wide sand bar to make camp for the night. The days were so long in Alaska in August that we were ready for bed long before dark.

He fixed a good meal of steak with trimmings. However, it became evident to me that he had minimal equipment. He planned to sleep with us in *our small tent*. I have never had an outfitter sleep with his clients!

He had no dining tent, or dining fly. He had no hip boots, as we had and very poor rain gear. In our corresponding he gave us a list of clothes and equipment that we needed but he must have been in a daze, since he listed so few items. Of course, in retrospect, his lack of experience was the cause of what would prove to be our extreme discomfort. Mark and I had hip boots, and light Gortex rain jackets with down liners. In addition, we had two changes of clothes.

We had two rods each, one light and one medium in weight. We had small lures, but few of the size that we would need later for Silver Salmon, that we hoped that we would find, when we reached the coast. Our main fish of interest for the trip would be the Silver Salmon. The small lures were perfect for the Grayling, Dolly Varden and Rainbow Trout. These three species on light tackle are a challenge to catch.

The next day dawned clear but with more clouds than the day before. However, by afternoon it began to rain, lightly at first and then more heavily. Sitting in the raft and fishing from the raft was great. We often caught fish while moving and landed them and turned them back without stopping. However, we often snagged, and if moving, lost our lures. We would stop regularly on the sand bars and fish up and down until bored and then move on.

We pitched camp in the rain that night. I began to weary of the rain in my face and everything being wet as we tried to eat and perform our regular camping chores. I was particularly concerned for our sleeping bags. I carefully wrapped each one in a large plastic garbage sack. I also put several more sacks in my pocket for future use. Rene did not tell us to have everything in rubber rain gear as is required by other outfitters, and as good sense would dictate. We camped on a sand bar. Our tent was about ten feet above the bar but Rene had all of his food items, stoves, chests, etc. right on the bar, including his leather hiking shoes. As we retired, I mentioned that he should move his gear higher on the sand bar, but he didn't pay any attention to me.

I awoke several times during the night to hear the rain and wind whipping on our small tent. It would sway back and forth but remained upright until morning. I arose, dressed, put on my rain gear and looked out. It was raining and looked as if it would rain forever. I looked at the river and it had risen about two feet higher than it was when we retired. I quickly ran to where all of our other gear was located. The water had risen and covered the smaller items on the sand bar. The chests and other gear were not harmed. But food and other items outside of containers were covered. Rene's hiking boots were covered. I didn't say anything to him but my concern for the rest of the trip began to increase.

We had a wet breakfast, since cooking in the rain was difficult and the tent was too small to use. We packed our gear and started off. The fishing was great. The rain did not matter and as we continued down the river, we began to catch beautiful Rainbows, some up to four and five pounds. I was fishing on a long strip of rapids, with large rocks and other great hiding places for trout.

I flipped my little Mepps spinner and it began to drift. Immediately, as the line tightened, something *large* took the lure and started straight across the river, which, by now was about fifty yards wide. As it reached the other side, I tried to follow it, since I could not turn it and then it started up stream. I started after it, slipping and falling on the rocks, but to no avail; it began to strip my line and soon the line was gone and so was the fish.

Primitive conditions while floating the Kanectok River didn't prevent "fishing fever." Note garbage sacks to help divert the rain out of our boots, Alaska, 1985.

I was fishing along a sand bank. The raft was beached and Rene was sitting on the edge, with a bored look on his face. He occasionally fished but not as much as Mark and I. As I worked my way down river, I looked down and saw my first spawned-out and dead King Salmon. For the Kanectok river is a great river for Kings. It must have been about 25 pounds. The eagles and other predators had began to devour it. As we traveled down the river, increasing numbers were found, until in places they appeared to be everywhere. They are dark red, almost black by this time. This area of the river appeared to be the ideal location for the laying of the eggs. In a few weeks, the Silver Salmon would appear there also, unless, for some reason, they laid their eggs in other areas along the river. We were about 80 miles upstream from the Pacific Ocean. As I looked at these huge fish, some up to 50 pounds, I wondered where they had been since their birth right there from 4-7 years before. They were born there, migrated to the Pacific Ocean and returned to the very location they were born, spawned and then died.

The river was much larger now and with the banks well cut and often up to two feet high. There were more trees along the stream bed, alders and other species that I did not recognize. They were not large, 20 to 30 feet high. The depth of soil on the shore was only a foot or less. The trees along the bank often blew over and lay straight across the river. They were called "sweeps" and needed to be watched very carefully by the oarsman of any raft going by. As we drifted, we had several near misses by the trees. We were going along and there was a sharp turn to the left. Mark yelled, "watch out, Dad," but it was too late, and a tree caught me and over I went into the river.

The water was extremely cold, but my concern for my safety was more than the shock of the cold water. The water was swift, but I swam and waded to the nearest sand bank. Rene tried to stop the raft but it was a couple of hundreds yards down river before he could beach the raft. Mark came running up to me and asked me how I was. I began to shake from the cold and told him to quickly get me a change of clothes, which he did. I dried and tried to put on the clothes before they became wet from the constantly falling rain.

Soon, we were back on the river. We would catch Dolly Varden and Rainbows until we became bored and then we would drift quietly in the rain. It was evident now that this was a very long flood plain and it was very flat. However, the river was running at a good rate and the constant rain had increased the flow. The water was slightly roily but it was not enough to affect the fishing.

When the rain would lighten, the mosquitoes would descend with a vengeance. Our repellent would work until the rain washed it off. We camped that night on another sand bar. I walked the sand bar and came across our first sign of the great Alaskan Brown Bear. One had walked the sand bar a few hundred feet below where our tent was pitched. I continued to watch to see that our sleeping bags did not get wet. That became a problem since they were only wrapped in garbage sacks.

Rene had a 12-gauge shotgun, with a cut-off barrel and a carrying strap. In Alaska, most of the guides used shotguns. A 12-gauge slug has more killing power, at very close range, than the larger caliber guns and so they were used for protection. We were in our sleeping bags that night and I was thinking about the bear that had walked by at some time in the past. "Rene, do you have your shotgun handy?" He replied, "yes, I placed it right by the tent door." Having learned something about Rene's behavior on this trip, I continued the questioning: "**Is the gun loaded?**" Long pause…"no, I don't think so." "Do you know where the shells are?" Long pause…"they are somewhere in our gear. I know that I have seen them since we started." I then retorted, "what do you intend to do, if a bear comes, beat it to death?"

The bear didn't come. I was so tired that I slept most of the night. When I did awake, I heard the rain off and on through the night. The next morning was about the same. The rain would come and go and so would the mosquitoes. I began to compare the rain with the mosquitoes but could not decide which one I preferred. This morning, I slipped out ahead of Mark and Rene. There was a long, deep hole along one side of the river with a rocky bar next to it. I began to catch those ravenous, aggressive, Dolley Varden.

I had caught eight and released them before Mark stuck his head out of the tent to see if he could take another day! I wanted to eat more fish.

We ate a Graying which was unimpressive. The Dollies were about like our Rainbows at home. Mark cooked a large Rainbow the last night we camped on the river with Rene. We could have eaten more but with the rain and no protection, cooking became a real chore.

We floated more and fished less during the morning. The rain continued on and off all day. About 2:00 we came to a part of the river with more sweeps than usual and Rene had to work harder to keep out of them. However, when the current was strong it pulled the raft into the bank in those locations. I was dozing, Mark yelled: "Watch out." The raft swung around and I saw this tree coming right at me. It was too low in the water for me to duck. I grabbed it as the raft went by. I was hanging on by both arms, at the end of it. The water was swift; the raft was already out of sight. The tree was teetering, since I was on the end of it, out about 20 feet from the bank. I thought, "this is not as bad as the last time, I will just work my was across the tree and climb on the bank."

The thought had no more than crossed my mind when I began to hear the tree crack. The tree had long since died, and was dry and brittle. Down I went. The water was deep and when I came up, my glasses, and hat were gone! The water was swift, so I kept upright and drifted until I could work my way to the nearest sand bar. Soon, here came Mark again. I immediately began to shake from the cold. The temperature was probably in the low 50's and being so wet, I was very uncomfortable.

I sent Mark back for my last dry change of clothes. There was no way to dry our clothes, or even to build a fire. The rain was incessant. I looked down by my feet. There was the largest pile of bear dung that I had ever seen! The brush was heavy along the bank. As I looked, I could imagine a bear coming out at any moment! I made my contingency plan, in case a bear would show…jump right back in the river and swim like hell! Mark returned with a towel and clothes. I dressed but continued to be cold and uncomfortable. I just could not seem to get my temperature back to normal.

We didn't fish much that afternoon. By 6:00, I began to get the chills and began to shake, lightly at first, but then more violently. I knew that I had the first symptoms of hypothermia. I told Rene that we would have to stop and camp soon. He was not very receptive but finally agreed. I explained my situation to Mark. He understood and we stopped. I had them set up the tent first. I ate a little cold food and then crawled into my dry sleeping bag and began to warm. I stayed awake until I was warm and then slept soundly the rest of the night.

The next morning, I began to review the situation. The fishing was great but our conditions were terrible. We had been in the rain for three or four days. I had been swept off the raft twice and had no more dry clothes. Our food was poor. We were constantly wet and uncomfortable. Rene, by this time, had began to be withdrawn, rude and would go hours without saying anything to us. I got Mark aside and told him that we were going to make all decisions for the balance of the trip.

The next morning I informed Rene that I would be making all decisions. I told him how I felt and that we should drift to the coast as fast as we could and that we would be doing little fishing until we reached the coast. He didn't say much. We packed and were on our way. We drifted as fast as we could. Rene worked very hard at the oars. The river was much larger by now and the threat from the sweeps was much less. We tried to stay in the middle of the river.

Rene had floated the river a couple of times but really was unfamiliar with it and he carried no maps. We were floating that afternoon and I looked ahead down the river and there was a float plane! We slowed and then we could see that a very nice fishing camp was located there. I motioned for Rene to stop at the camp. He did. These were Westport tents. Those were great tents, large, oval, with wood floors and aluminum interior supports. This was a "high dollar camp." There was a large cooking and lounging tent, sleeping tents, etc. We introduced ourselves to the outfitter. We explained our situation. He didn't have much to say, but offered us hot drinks and told us to get warm while we were there.

The hot drink was great and I worked my way to the heating stove. We began to feel much better. Most of the clients were out in various locations fishing for different species of fish. The clients were brought in by float plane and then the smaller boats were used for fishing. He told us we were about 20 miles above the coast.

I looked at the outfitter and he was wearing neoprene chest waders, with wading shoes. Although common now, they were new to me. I looked at them closely and made a vow that those would be what I would wear if I ever had the courage to go to Alaska again. Speaking of rain gear, Mark and I had expensive Gortex rain jackets but they were inadequate for the industrial strength rain that we were experiencing. These jackets were great for most conditions. But under constant heavy rain, they wicked up the sleeves and up the bottom. No salesman or clothier will admit this but I speak from experience. The best gear for this type of fishing is the old fashion rubber rain gear that is so common on commercial fishing boats. Needless to say, *now* I have all of the best gear for Alaska fishing.

I have mentioned above, that one seldom sees women fishing in those conditions. While we were in the dining tent, a large tall, blonde woman walked in, dressed in neoprene wading boots and all of the other necessary gear for Alaska. I introduced myself to her. She had come to Alaska from Sweden, by herself, to fly fish the Kanectock River. She appeared to be about 40 years old and, judging from our conversation, was a professional of some kind. We talked about fishing. She was charming, well educated, and spoke very good English. We stayed in the tent for about an hour. I expressed my great appreciation to the outfitter for his hospitality and information.

We continued down the river and within a few miles came upon another semi-permanent type of fishing camp. It was quite large. However, the clients from that camp came up from the coast, in large jet boats. We waved as we went by and continued down the river. When we were about five miles above the coast, we came upon the third camp. It appeared to be temporary, in nature, with smaller tents and boats. We waved as we went by.

By evening, we thought we were nearing the coast. Rene told us that at the mouth was a Native village called Quinhagak. The river was wide here and we drifted into a maze of islands and bays. Rene told us that we should be able to catch Silver Salmon here. So Mark and I got out and tried to wade and walk our way around. We found a couple of good holes. We lost several lures but did catch our first Silver Salmon. They were about 8-10 pounds each. But it was so hard to wade and the conditions were so difficult that I told Rene to camp for the night and that in the morning we would find our way to the village. Rene seemed to think that he knew where he was. But with drifting, we might miss the village and end up at the mouth of the river, not being able to get back up to the village.

In the morning, I felt better and was ready to catch some more Silvers! However, I had lost most of the lures that Rene had given us. He was supposed to supply us with these special lures. He didn't want to give us any more because he said that he was supposed to meet another group of clients at Quinhagak and needed the lures for them! This was about the end of our relationship with Rene. We packed and began to float on down the river. When we neared the village, it was easy to see where we should go. We had to row up a channel to the village. A small air strip was located at the village. There was a plywood shack at the strip. A native woman, with a phone to the chartered airline, served as sort of a representative of the company.

While Rene unloaded the gear and packed the raft for the flight out, Mark and I went down to the village where we learned that we could take a shower and clean up. I never remember a hot shower that felt so good! After we showered, we walked back. We had informed the "ticket agent," that we wanted a flight to Bethel where we could catch a scheduled plane back to Anchorage.

When we got back to the gravel airstrip, there were several other clients from one of the camps also waiting for the flight. One of the operators of the camp was named Bill Lyle. Mark struck up a conversation with him, and told him of our experiences. He was sympathetic. He said that the Silver Salmon fishing was great and that he had a three day opening in one of his small self-help camps. The rate was only $300. I told the ticket agent to cancel our flight!

In the meantime, Rene had packed the gear and carried it to the airstrip from the River. I had to settle our account with Rene. One of Rene's selling points for us going with him, since he was new, was a guarantee. He said that if we were not pleased, we would not have to pay. I had given him a down payment but that was a small part of the total cost. We talked about the guarantee. I told him all of my concerns and gave him a strong lecture with many useful suggestions. He was distraught. I was concerned for the next group of clients that he would be taking out. I thought about what was fair. I told him that I would give him 50% of the charges. He accepted the offer. The last time I saw Rene Limmeres, he was sprawled on his gear waiting for the next plane to take him back to Dillingham.

Bill Lyle told us to go to the village, get our gear washed and dried, pick up some lures and other things at the local general store and be back in a couple of hours. He would take us up the river to his camp. We had a new lease on life and on fishing! We washed and dried our clothes. We picked up some gear and were waiting at the river. Bill had some 20 foot john boats with jet engines and we were soon up the river at his camp. The camp was divided into two locations. A "high dollar" camp where everything was furnished, cooking, booze, Westport tents, etc.

Our camp was across and down the river. It had a sleeping and a cooking and lounging tent. I called our camp "the ghetto camp." Nothing looked better to Mark and me. We were delighted. All of the food and goodies were furnished. But we had to do our own cooking. The river was such that there were several good holes and we did not have to leave the general area. We cooked with propane, I asked Bill what a 100 pound bottle of propane cost delivered at the fishing camp. He said $100! I asked him what gasoline cost. He replied it cost $5 per gallon, in 55 gallon drums.

Bill left us there and told us he would be back in a few hours. We settled in and soon were fishing. We caught a few fish that we thought were Silvers and released them. Later, we saved what we thought were Silver Salmon. They looked a little different, however. They were not as bright and had a purple color which looked like someone painted their sides with water color and it ran down the sides.

Later that evening Bill came back to help us. He laughed when we showed him our fish. We had been catching Chum Salmon, which were running with the Silvers. They were also called Dog Salmon and are generally considered inferior to the Silvers. I could not understand that. They hit and fought equally or better than the Silvers. Later on, I would eat them and could not tell the difference. But, we were determined that we would catch Silvers.

Bill gave us a ten minute demonstration on how to use large Mepps spinners or Pixies and we soon found that we could do very well. We released all of them since we had no way to refrigerate them until we would leave. Bill taught us many things that would be so useful for future trips with him and to other parts of Alaska.

Bill Lyle's fishing camp produced outstanding Silver Salmon, Alaska, 1985.

The second afternoon, Bill told us to take our cooler and figure out how many fish it would take to fill it and be prepared to send the cooler out on the next plane. It would be put in a freezer at the village. We would pick it up when we flew out and it would be considered luggage and we would not have to pay freight.

The second afternoon, Mark and I decided to catch and prepare our fish to take home. We figured about 12 or so would fill the cooler. It didn't take us very long to catch them and they were in an impressive row on a sand bar. It was about 8:00 p.m. Bill came by and asked us if we were finished with the hole for the night. We told him yes. He said he would be back. We didn't realize it at the time, but we had one of the best holes in the whole area to catch Silvers.

Soon, Bill and his business partner returned. I do not recall his name. I soon realized that they both had been drinking heavily. They wanted to have a "fishing contest." We said that while they were fishing we would continue to prepare our fish. They were fishing with wet flies. The bet was the winner would get $100 and $1 for each fish caught more than the loser. To count, the fish would have to be brought to the sand bar and released.

We watched the action. I have never heard such yelling, cursing and carrying on! This went on for a little over an hour when they decided to end the contest. Results: the winner caught 108 and the loser 100. Therefore the winner received $108. I mention this story to illustrate the number and quality of fish on this river at that time.

The rain continued but we had such comforts that we didn't complain. We had a problem with the rain. Our jackets were not long enough to go over our hip boots and they funneled the rain water right into our boots. One morning Mark got an idea. We took two large plastic garbage sacks, cut holes for head and arms and pulled them down over our boots. Problem solved! We may have looked strange but who cared?

Our day of departure dawned clear and sunny. We had a great time. I lost count of the Silvers caught and released. We ate well. We had good outfitters. This part of the experience on the Kanectok River helped make up for the days when we were so uncomfortable. However, the great fishing on that float trip is remembered *almost* as much as the discomfort.

Our flight back to Bethel was on time and uneventful. We returned with 70 pounds of premium fish. Bill took us to the airstrip. I expressed our enjoyment for the time spent in his camp. I told him that we would return again. Bill invited us to return the next June for King Salmon. I did return but that is another story…

Cabela's New Rod Design

During the winter of 1986, I contacted a severe case of fishitis. This was brought on by a somewhat successful fishing trip in Alaska the previous August. I have already told you about the famous float trip with Mark down the Kanectoc River. I called Bill Lyle, an outfitter in Anchorage and asked him about fishing for King Salmon. He gave me the usual sales pitch and I was hooked. I booked a trip for myself for June of the next year.

During the summer of 1986, I worked on all of the equipment that I knew that I would need for the trip. My experiences of the previous summer made a permanent and lasting effect on my being fully prepared. I had neoprene chest waders, better rain gear and wading shoes. However, I later found that I like the waders with their own attached shoes. The other type developed leaks from having sand settle into the shoes.

I ordered a special medium weight fishing rod from the famous Cabela's store in Nebraska. That was before they built their new super store in Sidney, Nebraska. This rod captured my attention. It carried the Cabela's name so I knew it would be good. It was a tapered graphite rod, medium weight, with a new adaptation where the handle of the reel fit up into the rod itself. What a unique idea! I took this rod and another medium weight rod and scores of lures that Bill told me to bring. I bought them by the dozen! In that river, snags were so common that many of them were lost.

My booking was for the third week of June. In fact, through the years, on the Kanectok River, June 21 was the best day for King Salmon Fishing. Although the salmon runs vary in time, caused by different conditions, June 21 was best.

I flew to Anchorage on Northwest Airlines, then to Bethel on Alaska Airlines and then on to Quinhagak on a small chartered line. I had a hard time containing my excitement from Bethel to the small native village. I had never seen the tundra and the flood plain so beautiful. The colors from above were indescribable. Such unique pastel colors of green and blues and in some places various hues of reds and purples. Thousands of lakes and small rivulets appeared as far as the eye could see.

Several of us were flying to Quinhagak that day. I was sitting next to a woman and we visited. She was also going fishing in one of Bill Lyle's camps up the river. Her husband was already fishing and she was going to join him. She was a nurse from Anchorage. I said goodbye to her when we landed, thinking that I probably would never see her again.

In the summer, in this area, there is absolutely no other way to travel except by air. The winter is different. In much of Alaska, the rivers become the highways and they are used extensively with snowmobiles.

Bill was waiting for me at the airstrip. The plywood shack was still there. However, someone had broken in and it was full of junk, mostly beer and whisky containers. We placed my gear in the boat and roared up the river in the jet boat. Jets are used instead of regular motors because they can operate in more shallow water.

I stayed in the "high dollar camp" this time. We had a person who Bill had hired as a cook, but that title was highly complimentary. But who has to eat when the fish are biting? It was late afternoon by the time I got there. There were several others in the camp with their own party. I was alone, except for the attention that Bill gave me. I settled in and spent the evening fishing. I didn't get a single bite! I was a little discouraged, having caught so many fish the past summer. However, those were King Salmon! Fish are different in size in the different rivers. They run at different times and the fisherman must be aware of when they are in the rivers working their way up to spawn and die.

Time would prove that the Kings were more prevalent in the Kanectok River than in some of the more famous rivers like the Kenai, but they were not as large. The largest Kings and the record Kings are from the Kenai. However, that river is so accessible to fisherman that the fish are under great pressure and the regulations are very severe.

The next morning I prepared my new rod. Bill looked and laughed at me. He said: "are you going to fish for Kings with that rod?" I was a little insulted and said, "if there are any in this river, I will catch them with this rod." I walked up river to a large hole and began to cast. There was an old man from our camp fishing across the hole.

I put on a 2-ounce pixie and whipped it out into the middle of the river and began to retrieve it. When it came back about half way, *wham,* and my first King had struck my lure. I set the hook as best I could. Kings have very hard mouths and the hooks have to be set well or they will escape. Large Kings don't often break water but the smaller ones often do. This one came out and danced for me. I was excited as I tried to set my drag and prepare for the fight. I knew my gear was light for Kings but I always use lighter gear than most other fishermen. The fish are not kept, so my philosophy is to increase the challenge!

This King appeared to be about 25 pounds, indeed later, it proved to be 25 pounds. My medium rod was almost doubled as I tried to tire this fish out. Then all of a sudden, something happened. I looked down and my rod was in my right hand and my reel was in my left hand and the fish was having a fit right in front of me. It started to run and the line tightened so much you could have used it for a violin string. I began to panic.

The old man across the hole was watching me. I yelled; "can you help me?" He dropped his rod and came running over with a net. He was one of the few fishermen to use a net but it was a welcome sight to me. Had

I known how many Kings I would catch on that trip, I would not have been so concerned. I handled the rod and he handled the reel and we landed that fish. My first King Salmon! One of my favorite photos is the one taken when we finally finished the job.

Cabela's rod broke, but my spare rod saved me and several King Salmon, Alaska, 1987.

I wound the balance of the line on to the reel and headed for camp to use my other rod. I looked at the rod and the sleeve that was supposed to hold the reel in place and noticed that it was made of graphite. It was obvious that it needed to be brass or steel! I didn't say anything to Bill about changing rods.

More salmon came into the rivers at high tide than any other time. Of course, many will remain in certain areas of the river resting. They do not feed after entering fresh water. When they strike various lures and flies, it is not for food. Other motivations cause this behavior. Pinks and Sockeye seldom strike at all and, in spite of game and fish regulations and the hype from guides and outfitters, most landed are snagged by one method or another.

Therefore, fishing will vary from hour to hour, based on the latest tide and the number of fish moving up the rivers. After I returned to the river after exchanging rods, I caught four or five more that day. I usually averaged five to ten a day, sometimes more. More dedicated fishermen often caught and released scores in one day, under optimum conditions.

Toward the end of the week, during the middle of the day, I was resting in my bunk when I heard a jet boat coming down the river. This did not surprise me since Bill came and went during the day. Natives would often travel up and down the river for various reasons. Occasionally, natives would stop at the camp and ask for food or alcohol. We would give them food but never any alcohol.

I heard the jet boat land near our camp. Suddenly Bill Lyle yelled: "Hey, Mahaffey come down here. I want to show you something." I put on my waders and other gear and strolled down to the river. There was Bill with the nurse that I had met a few days earlier. She was returning to Anchorage and was taking some fish with her. She had coolers ready to fill after Bill filleted the fish.

I looked at the bottom of the john boat. There must have been eight or ten large Kings, averaging 30 pounds, more or less. Bill had a cutting board on the sand bar and was soon making huge fillets from those fish and placing them in the coolers. I watched with interest as the fish disappeared from the bottom of the boat.

Another fish began to appear underneath those on top. This fish was the last one in the boat. I walked over and looked at it. It was incredibly large. I asked: "Have you weighed that fish?" Bill said: "Yes, it weighs 70 pounds." He climbed into the boat to lift it out. It was the largest King I had ever seen, except for three or four mounted in the Anchorage Hotels.

I turned to the woman and said: "You are not going to fillet that beautiful fish, are you? Aren't you going to have it mounted?" She replied: "No, we are going to eat it. We have a photo of it." Bill carefully took the trophy and laid it on the cutting board. I had to walk away, so that tears would not come, as he butchered that gorgeous fish.

Supposedly, the most popular eating salmon is the Sockeye. They average 8-10 pounds and are deep orange in color. The Pink is the primary commercial fish caught. It is the salmon that you buy in cans. The Chum or Dog Salmon is not considered a good eating salmon, although I could not tell it from a Silver. The Chinook or King Salmon is my favorite. It has more oil in it than the other salmon and I like an oily fish. I especially like commercially grown catfish, because it is also an oily fish. The reason the Chum is called Dog Salmon is because, traditionally, the natives fillet and dry these fish to feed to their sled dogs.

I have seen scores of these fish on drying racks in various native villages. They split them in half, bone them and lay them on the racks. If you travel Alaska you will see a lot of sled dogs around some homes but they are seldom used. The natives use snowmobiles! But they continue to keep the dogs although they don't use them. I have seen as many as 15-20 dogs on separate stakes around one house. Some dogs may have various types of shelters.

Later in the week Bill took me up the river to fish in a different hole. We went by jet boat. It was difficult to walk along the river for any distance and some of the better holes were widely separated. He dropped me off and said that he would pick me up later. There was another fisherman who had already been dropped off. He was from our camp, but I had not met him. He was a psychiatrist from San Francisco. He was in his early seventies and loved to fish! Since I was a loner on this trip, I was anxious to have some companionship.

He was a neat guy. He was one of the few psychiatrists or psychologists that I have met that didn't need one. Perhaps, it was fishing that "normalized" him. I have often thought that he should have prescribed fishing for some of his disturbed patients. He could have told them how President Herbert Hoover felt about fishing:

"Fishing is the chance to wash one's soul with pure air. It brings meekness and inspiration, reduces our egotism, soothes our troubles and shames our wickedness. It is discipline in the equality of men—for all men are equal before fish."

The New York Herald Tribune (May 19, 1947)

This was to be my last day fishing on this trip. I wanted to harvest some fish to take back. Waiting until the last minute to save fish was a little risky but is better than letting them spoil before getting them back home. So we began to save our fish. Several were small, 18-20 pounds with a few 30 pounders. We lined them on the bank. After we had all that we needed we began to release them as we did most of the time. The doctor was fishing to my right, standing on a high bank, and casting off from it. I was afraid that he would fall as he climbed down the bank, trying to release these fish. So, I volunteered to release his fish for him. He caught several and I began to spend as much time helping him as I did in my own fishing.

Above, Bill Lyle, butchering the trophy King Salmon. Below, the psychiatrist with his 56-pound King Salmon, Alaska, 1987.

I was down to my last few green pixies. He had no pixies. He was using a large alligator lure. This was a very large silver spoon. I was flipping my pixie into the middle of the river when he yelled: "I've got another one on. He feels like a good one." This was not news to me by now. I yelled back and told him that I would be ready when the fish was played out. I looked at him occasionally in the next 20 minutes and he was working back and forth and up and down the bank, one time nearly falling into some willows.

After about 25 minutes, he yelled: "I think that he's ready to land now." I reeled in my lure, dropped my rod and walked down the bank. He was standing above and behind me. I looked into the water and exclaimed: "He's as big as a submarine. Let me try to weigh him. What do you want to do with him." The old man responded, "He's too big to keep, let's let him go."

I had just purchased a new, expensive brass fish scale and I had it in my tackle box. The big fish was beached, but was still mostly under water. I told my companion that I would need some help in weighing him. He worked his way down the bank and helped me. The fish scale went to 50 pounds but had marks beyond to about 60 pounds. I finally got the hook in the fish and weighed him. I had to extrapolate beyond the 50 pounds and estimated the fish weighed 56 pounds! What a fish! This was the largest fish that I had watched anyone catch.

I wanted to keep him for fillets but the old man said we should turn him back. I told him that I thought we had already killed him. So we tried to revive him. I climbed into the river and straightened him up and rocked him back and forth for a few minutes, working the water through his gills. Soon, I felt a shiver of life and then it took off like a submarine toward the middle of the river. We both gave sighs of relief and sat down to rest and have a bite to eat. Time was passing and I knew that Bill would soon be back and my fishing would be over for another trip. I looked at the fish lined up ready to fillet. What a sight. Only in Alaska.

In an hour or so I heard the boat coming and knew that it was about over. The old man only had one Alligator lure. He had another two or three days of fishing. I looked into my tackle box and found three green pixies. (I never ordered green ones, they were sent by mistake. I usually used the orange ones. I had lost all of them and had been reduced to green. However, they worked fine).

Bill beached the boat and I put in all of our fish. Bill told the old man that he would be back to pick him up later. I quietly walked back, told the doctor that I enjoyed fishing with him that day. I took his hand and placed those pixies in it. He looked at me, tears formed in his eyes. We hugged and I climbed into the boat. I had a strange but warm feeling as the jet boat hummed its way back to camp.

Bill took me to the airstrip and dropped me off. He knew that I could wait by myself. He helped me lift all of my gear and two coolers full of King fillets. I sat on the gear and listened as Bill started the jet boat and taxied up the canal and then I heard him open it up and head for camp.

I was soon back in Bethel, then Anchorage and finally Kansas City. On this trip, I went to Kansas City but my fish went to Denver. However, I retrieved the coolers the next day and everything turned out great.

After I returned home I put all of my gear away, with the hopes of making another trip. I took the Cabela rod out of my rod case and looked at it again. Definitely, a design error. I placed it aside, with the intention of taking it back to the Cabela store in Kearney, Nebraska.

I forgot about the rod. Three years later, I was preparing for a trip west to Salt Lake City via Interstate #80. I had a couple of pairs of pants that did not fit and I was going to return them and visit the store. I have always been impressed with the return policy of Cabela's store. Their "satisfaction or your money back," is a literal policy. I have taken many items back, mostly because of a wrong size. However, one time I purchased a pair of kangaroo hunting boots. The tops were perfect, but the soles appeared to be melting away for some reason. It became apparent that there was something wrong with the rubber compound. I took them back and the store pro-rated them without a hassle. Then I remembered the rod, as it broke, that had given me such a panic attack when the 25-pound King Salmon attacked my Pixie on the Kanectok River. I would return the rod, with the pants, on the way to Salt Lake City.

Visiting a Cabela store is an experience. The *old store* is located on the northeast side of Kearney on old Highway #30. Many times I have made the turn north and watched as the large water tower loomed ahead as a beacon to the mecca of hunting and fishing supplies. There is more than a store in Kearney. It is the headquarters of the mail order business for the large company. The retail sales is a mere fraction of the total sales made by mail and now by internet. There are many buildings there and the traffic and other activities indicate the size of the total operation.

I never stop at the old store any more, even though I usually take Interstate #80 back and forth several times each year. There is now a *new store!* It is located close to Interstate #80, at Sidney, Nebraska, about a 100 miles east of Cheyenne, Wyoming. It looms on the horizon, coming from either direction, like a giant arena. At first, there was only the store, but now a small city is developing around the activities that the store generates.

It is more than a store, it is a *wildlife museum,* with several million dollars worth of mounted fish and wildlife specimens. It is one of the major tourist attractions in Nebraska and might generate the most visitation in the state. The store is large, with an incredible inventory of any item that a hunter or fisherman would need. One attraction is the "Cave," a special room where all returns are offered to the buyer at a discount off the new price. When I stop, I always plan on at least an hour and a half for my visit, most of which is *wishing* as I view the displays of goods *and* mounted fish and animals.

But, back to returning my defective rod at the old store in Kearney. It was early in the morning, the store had just opened, and there were no other customers at the return desk. I exchanged the pants with no difficulty. I then handed the rod to the clerk and said: "I want to return this rod, it's defective." The clerk picked it up and looked at it. It appeared that he had never seen this new concept of inserting the handle of the reel into the handle of the rod. He had no problem recognizing it as a Cabela rod since it had the name all over it.

"Now, what seems to be the problem," he asked. I showed him the place where the reel was inserted. The graphite cover, that held the reel in place, looked about normal, with a slight indentation where the reel had sprung loose. I said: "This won't hold the reel in place, if a large King Salmon attacks your Pixie in the middle of the Kanectok River in Alaska."

The clerk said: "It looks okay to me, I don't think it's defective." I rolled my eyes and thought, "How can I convince this guy that this rod is defective?" I then decided that I would tell him the whole story. I started with getting on the plane in Kansas City and then getting on the plane in Anchorage and then getting on the plane at Bethel. By now, a few people had started to line up behind me and were listening intently. I was just about to get into the boat at Quinhagak, when the clerk sighed and said: "You've convinced me. How much did you pay for it? Do you have a receipt?" "No, I bought it several years ago, and I don't have a receipt," I replied.

The clerk began to punch in numbers into the computer-register and it was cranking and grinding away. I am not sure that the clerk ever got the right number attached to that rod, but finally he said: "How does $45 sound?" I couldn't remember what I paid for it but replied, "that's okay with me." Then I remembered that old adage that says: "*It's not the principle, it's the money that counts.*"

Caribou Have White Feet

I can get excited and emotional about hunting and fishing. I wish that I had the time and patience to write about every experience, but alas, this would take a lot of paper and the reader might become bored!

I do want to write about the only hunting trip that I have made to Alaska. This was made in late August of 1993. I went with Robert Ruude, whom I sometimes refer to as Fat Bob, who was a Bellman Propane customer with whom I became acquainted. This was, actually, a combination hunting and fishing trip. We timed the early caribou hunt with the latest Silver Salmon run.

Certain game animals, and fish for that matter, can be harvested in different ways. This is true for elk, deer, antelope and caribou. There are local herds, migrating herds and scattered small groups of all of these animals.

Fat Bob and I had gone to the southwest part of Alaska, near the Becharof National Wildlife Refuge. It was also near Katmai National Monument. In fact, I had fished the national park on another trip there; I fished out of one of the more famous fishing lodges. But that trip we fished lower down near the wildlife refuge. We became acquainted with the guide and outfitter. He seemed competent so we booked a caribou hunt for the following season. It must be remembered that all transportation is by plane; either float plane or wheel plane. Most of the better outfitters have both types of planes.

During the 1950's one of the large national oil companies had spent considerable time and money in oil exploration for about a 50-mile area.

There was no oil discovered and the company abandoned all of the buildings and left one road of about 40 miles. Very remote country. Abandoned buildings, canneries, lodges, and every type of debris are scattered all over Alaska. It is one of the great environmental tragedies.

This outfitter had taken some of the main oil company buildings and converted them to a primitive hunting and fishing lodge. Very austere but adequate. Who needs fancy accommodations while hunting or fishing? The food was great. The outfitter's mother was the cook on both trips that I made to the area. We slept in small rooms on bunk beds. There was a one hole privy. But we had hot water for a shower and a small dining room.

We had a choice of how to hunt. We could use 4 x 4 trucks using what was left of the road and hunt the more common method of spot and stalk…or we could be dropped off on the side of a remote mountain and look for small herds of large bachelor bull caribou.

Those caribou did not migrate from the area, except when the larger migrating herds of cows would go by. They would then move into the herds, breed the cows, stay for a time and then retreat from them into very remote areas. I had never heard of such animal behavior!

It didn't take us long to decide we wanted to hunt on the side of that remote mountain. A very small spike camp had been set up on the mountain before our arrival. We were taken in by a Super Cub with large wheels capable of landing and taking off in the rocks. We landed on a small volcanic strip of a couple of hundred feet!

In Alaska, it is illegal to hunt the same day that you fly into an area. This is to protect the animals from unfair harvesting. So, we flew into the camp in the afternoon. It was a beautiful afternoon, clear, warm and exciting. We set up a spotting scope and looked for game intermittently through the long afternoon and evening. The days were still very long. We spotted a few scattered cow caribou with calves. One came within a few hundred yards of our tent.

We had our dinner. I was not anxious to go into the tent. It was small, cramped and uncomfortable. I would look for game every 30 minutes or so to reduce the boredom. There was a beautiful creek nearby but we didn't bring our light fishing gear! I doubt that creek has ever been fished in that area!

I was looking northwest at some canyons, when I saw a large animal rise up and slowly move up a hill. It looked like a buffalo. Of course, I knew it wasn't a buffalo. So I asked our guide to look. He became excited and said it was one of the largest Alaska Brown Bears that he had seen in that area! In fact, that spring he had harvested a bear himself and it wasn't as large as the one we were viewing.

Later in the evening, the guide spotted a caribou bull about four miles to the northwest of us. It looked promising for the next day. Night finally came and I reluctantly went to bed in the small tent. I slept well, but awoke early and heard the rain pelting the tent. There is a saying in Alaska that you must plan to do everything in the rain or don't go to Alaska.

It rained hard all day! I would go out occasionally but with the fog and water on everything, it was very unpleasant. Nothing could be seen in the spotting scope. It also became cold and uncomfortable in the tent. I also learned that one doesn't want to be in a small tent with Robert Ruude! However, we prevailed. I suggested several times that we hunt an area close to camp. The guide would not consider it.

The morning of the next day was the same. I informed the guide that I would not spend another day in that tent with Fat Bob and that we were going to hunt! He reluctantly agreed that we would try to do some hunting. The rain slowly stopped but the fog remained. However, by mid-morning the fog lifted and we began to use the spotting scope again. The guide spotted what he believed to be the same caribou bull in the same general area.

We decided to make a stalk. It was between 3-4 miles from our camp. Fat Bob was overweight and couldn't walk far. He said that this would probably be his only stalk. I told him he could have the bull and I would go with him.

Unless one is familiar with the country, the terrain between the animal being stalked and camp is totally unknown. And so it was...canyons and a large creek had to be crossed. Fat Bob and I had on hiking boots but not waterproof. Fortunately the guide had on waterproof boots. So I convinced him to take us across the creek on his back...which he did in good humor. I knew if I got my boots that wet, I would be crippled before returning to camp. We used the spotting scope after we had walked about a mile. As we looked, there were two bulls instead of one. On receiving this news, I became much more motivated!

We continued our stalk across several more canyons and another small creek. We set up our scope again about a half mile from where the bulls were last spotted. The two bulls had now become four bulls! The two largest looked the same and the others were slightly smaller. I looked at the two largest and they were very symmetrical. Caribou antlers are seldom symmetrical, and although large, are not as attractive as elk antlers. The shovels, located in front are often very warped and unattractive, at least in my opinion.

We continued our stalk, much more cautiously now. As we neared the anticipated area, alder trees became prominent along the draw. They were about 10-15 feet high and bushy. We found a high hill to look into the draw where they had been. We needed no optics at this point. *The bulls were no where to be seen!*

The wind was in our favor. The guide was confident we had not spooked them. But where were they? I climbed the nearest high hill but could not see them. We decided that we would work through the alders down a long ridge. Stalking was easy since the rain had softened up the ground and we made no noise. Suddenly we looked ahead and crossing from left to right, we saw huge antlers moving up and down through the alder branches. What a sight that was.

I had told Fat Bob that he could have the first shot so he was behind the guide and I was last. They moved off to the right and I worked straight ahead. We didn't know that there was a steep draw about 50 feet deep running at an angle to where the bulls were moving. Suddenly I found myself right on the edge of the canyon. I looked down below the Alders and I saw eight white feet! I suddenly learned that **Caribou have white feet.**

Top, an unusually symmetrical set of caribou antlers. Middle, head, capes and quarters had to be carried to the nearest landing point. Below, several trips were needed to remove caribou antlers and quarters, Alaska, 1993.

I looked behind me for the others. No where in sight! I quickly retreated until I found them and motioned that I had found the bulls. We all ran down the trail to the edge of the canyon. All four bulls had moved the full length of that draw and were at the end of it, where it made a sharp angle to the right. They saw us and were beginning to mill around. I told Fat Bob: "shoot or I will!" He took the largest and shot it square behind the shoulder. It turned completely around and he shot it in the same location on the other shoulder. It went down. I was confused. I asked the guide which was the other largest one. He said the one running to the right. I quickly got off a shot just before it went out of sight. Down it went. I could see the water splatter as the 165-grain .30-06 hit it in the middle of the spine.

My bull was about 50 yards from Fat Bob's bull. Two beautiful animals harvested at the same time. The guide began to dress them and to cape out the heads. The guide told me to go up on the nearest ridge to see if I could find a landing spot for the plane to come and pick up the meat.

I began my search. As I climbed the ridge, I saw a lot of large bear sign and then remembered this was the general area that we had seen the huge animal the first night in camp. I found what I thought was a strip long enough for the small plane to land about a half mile from the bulls.

Together we all carried the quartered animals to the landing site. I was a little worried about leaving the beautiful antlers there until the plane could pick them up. But they were not disturbed. After all of the work, we rested, had lunch and began our long trek back to camp.

The small Super Cub made several trips to get the animals and us back to the main camp. The antlers had to be tied on the wing struts and one animal at a time was flown out.

We still had several days to fish for Silver Salmon. We were flown out each day to a new place. We caught many Silvers. My oldest son Mark had made me a very light rod, almost ultra light. One day, I thought I would see if I could land one of the 10-12 pound Silvers on that rod. I landed two! But, what work! I was pleased to get back to a medium weight rod to handle all of the antics they perform while landing.

The large number of bears amazed me. I wanted to return to get one of the large Alaskan Brown Bears but have never had the opportunity. However, Robert Ruude did return later and killed a large Alaska Brown Bear in that area. I was confident that I would return to hunt bear. I even purchased a Ruger .375 H&H Magnum but have never used it.

I was anxious to return home and tell Barbara about all of our experiences. She met me at the door, her hands on her hips, and that look on her face that was so familiar to me: "Well, what did you bring back this time: dead fish, dead animals and dirty clothes?"

The Honeymoon Hunt

Hunting and fishing have affected my life in so many different ways. Why if it wasn't for a mule deer hunt that I had with Bob Knoble in October, 1953, I may not have met my wife, Barbara. We were all poor in those days. I was an apprentice printer at an hourly wage of $.96. That computes to be $2,000/year. Why now, practically everyone makes $2,000/week.

The local locker plants charged $5 to cut and wrap an antelope; $7 for a deer; and $20 for an elk. My problem was that I didn't have the $5. Bob didn't either, so we decided to cut up our own deer and freeze it. We purchased the freezer wrap. Bob had all of the necessary knives but we needed a meat saw. I suggested to use a carpenter's saw but Bob said we needed a meat saw. So, I began to seek one out.

I was working at the *Casper Tribune-Herald* at the time. One of the journeyman printers there was a man by the name of Lynn "Frosty" Frost. I had worked with him for a couple of months but didn't know him. In fact, he was a man of few words. He had been a Marine in WWII. He was on Wake Island, suffered the Battaan Death March, and was then sent to China to work in the coal mines. I might not have talked much either, had I suffered through those experiences.

Someone told me that Frosty had a meat saw. He said that I could borrow it. I went to the house and borrowed the meat saw from his wife, Mary, who was to be my future mother-in-law. Of course, I didn't know that at the time, or I probably would have found the $5 and had the deer processed!

We did a pretty good job of cutting up the meat. I ate it all winter. Then I remembered that I had to return the meat saw. I took the saw and a package of steaks as a thank you gift to Frosty's house. I remember it well. I walked up to the front porch, knocked on the door and waited. At this time I didn't know that Mary had twin daughters, although you would never guess the girls were twins from looking at them.

Millie, the larger of the two, and fortunately, the one that I didn't marry, answered the door. I stated my business and she took the saw and the package of steaks. I looked beyond her into the front room and…there she was…BARBARA ALICE PROUD. She was sitting on one of those old green, Naugahyde hassocks, the large style, about the size of one of those tubs they used to have elephants sit on for circus shows.

I looked closely. She was sitting on the hassock, sideways to me. She was dressed in denim pants, rolled up to her knees, a tight fitting blouse that gave the promise of an hour-glass figure, if she would stand up, which she didn't, unfortunately. On her tiny feet was a pair of black and white saddle oxfords, the rage of the time. In her hand was a telephone, into which she was rapidly conversing. Millie and I completed our conversation. Barbara never even looked up. But it was too late. I had been exposed to a PROUD girl and I would never be the same.

I began dating Barbara in November of that year. We went to movies, to lunch and I was over at her house a lot. There was no television in those days. She was a little skeptical of me but she liked my new car, a 1953 Chevrolet Coupe, with all of the neat accessories. At about this time I met a new linotype operator by the name of Terry Beaver, who had come up from Nebraska to fill a vacancy on the staff of the *Casper Morning Star* printed by the same company as the newspaper where I worked.

Terry and I became friends and eventually shared an apartment, where we cooperatively cooked and tried to figure out, by spring, how we could make that deer taste better. In the meanwhile, I continued to date Barbara. By early summer, Mary and Frosty were becoming concerned about my increasingly close association with their 16-year-old daughter. Having lived a long time since then and having reared three sons, they had good reason to be concerned.

By mid-summer, Mary was becoming increasingly critical of me. One night we had an argument and I realized that our courtship might be over. I gave it a lot of serious thought. I was five years older than she, had been in the military and was a lot more mature. I was confident, in my naivete, that I was capable of taking care of her. I asked her to marry me, she, in her naivete, accepted. Youth is a great time of life. Enthusiasm usually overwhelms good sense.

I knew that I couldn't ask Frosty for her hand or any other part of her body for that matter. Just thinking about asking Mary was frightening. So we decided that we would have to elope. I was in-experienced so I asked Terry to help. He didn't know any more than we did, but he was brave enough to research the surrounding states to see which would be the best one in which to get married.

New Mexico was the state of choice. Eighteen was the minimum age and there was no 3-day waiting period for a blood test. Barbara looked 18 years old, but we didn't have anything to prove that she was that age. We needed Terry again. He took her driver's license, and with a process still unknown to me, altered it to show that she was 18 years old. During the past half century, there have been times I have blessed him and cursed him for his competence in forging documents.

On Friday, August 13, we drove to Raton, New Mexico. The ceremony cost $13 and we drove 1300 miles on the trip. Since that time, I have been cautious when dealing with the number 13. We returned and I rented a tiny apartment. I borrowed $65 for the first month's rent.

October came and deer season was coming up. Terry asked if I wanted to go hunting. I said yes. We decided that we would go out and camp two days over the weekend. We decided to go out where I had hunted for years with my Step-Dad, Dave since I knew the area pretty well.

Then, I remembered my bride. I also made a serious mistake. I invited her along. I hadn't gotten over the togetherness attraction that newly married couples often have. Terry reluctantly said: "Okay," as he muttered something about women and hunting not mixing. We planned to go in my car.

We didn't have much camping equipment. I borrowed a tent and all of the other gear was primitive: no propane light or stove, or down sleeping bags or chairs. The weekend came. It was warm, dry and very windy as we found a dry camp site on the side of a sparsely timbered ridge.

Barbara and I cooked the evening meal on the first night. We had raw potatoes, cold string beans and burned minute steaks. Now it wasn't all Barbara's fault. Using sagebrush and Pinyon Pine is not the best fuel, especially when there were wind gusts approaching 40 mph, accompanied with dust and grit. "How do you keep out of the smoke," Barbara asked. "I don't know, just get used to it," I responded.

Darkness came, the fire was going out, and so we thankfully went into the tent out of the wind and out of the smoke. Terry had his sleeping bag. I had borrowed a double sleeping bag from Bob Knoble. We didn't have any mattresses or foam pads as we do now. I climbed in and Barbara followed. She was silent for a few minutes and then she said: "There's a lump under my back." I said: "don't worry about it, it's probably a rock. You'll get used to it." I was just about to doze off when she said: "I want to change places with you." I said: "*Why?*" She responded: "I'm going to let you get used to this rock."

In the morning, I helped with breakfast. I was under the impression that Barbara was going to stay in camp, perhaps sit in the car and read a book while we hunted. She said: "I'm going with you." I didn't have much choice so she and I went in one direction and Terry, fortunately, got to go in the other direction.

We hiked over a couple of ridges and Barbara asked: "Why aren't we seeing any deer?" I said that we might have to walk a long ways before seeing one. "What's a long ways?" she countered. "Oh, see all of those ridges along the skyline and then across that other valley," I responded. We climbed two of the ridges before she wanted to go back. We did see a doe and a fawn but that was not enough of an incentive for her to keep walking.

We got back to camp about noon. I ate a bite of lunch. Barbara disappeared into the tent. I started back in the general direction where we had been hunting and spent the rest of the afternoon on those ridges. Terry and I returned about the same time. Neither of us had seen a buck.

I solved the evening meal problem. We had cold cuts and a hot drink. I was so tired I didn't even feel the rock in the middle of my back. Barbara didn't respond in the morning as Terry and I got up, had breakfast and started hunting together.

Above, the honeymoon couple camping while hunting mule deer, Wyoming, 1954. Below, Terry Beaver and author with the two bucks shot in a box canyon.

We hunted most of the morning. Then we jumped two bucks, a small 4 x 4 and a smaller 3 x 3. The deer were trapped in a box canyon and had to go straight up to escape us. We started shooting at them as they bounded up the ridge. I can't remember how many shots it took but, after the smoke cleared, we could see that both were down before they reached the top.

Terry and I have been arguing for four decades about which person shot which animal. By now I can't remember and neither can he but we still disagree. We had a long, long ways to drag those two animals. It took the rest of the second day to get them to the car. By the time we packed those deer and all of the gear and three people in that coupe, it was full.

We were about to leave. Barbara looked at me and asked: "Is this it?" "Is this what?" I responded. "Is this what deer hunting is all about?" I said: "Oh, no, this is one of the better trips." In retrospect, that was one of the most important hunting trips of my life. Barbara has never asked to go with me again. While I am hunting, she just takes her credit card and visits the nearest mall.

Other Memorable Experiences

When considering a lifetime of hunting and fishing experiences, some are permanently recorded and others are long forgotten unless brought back to mind in some manner. The unsuccessful hunts are forgotten first! Some hunts are ruined by a poor companion. I have hunted with a lot of men…Once! I have had bird hunts ruined by other hunters' poor dogs. I have had fishing trips ruined by poor natured companions, equipment breaking down, boat motors stopping, etc.

I would like to record a few hunting and fishing trips that stand out in my mind for different reasons…

Second Chance

I worked for the U.S. Forest Service, on the Coconino National Forest, from 1964-1967. I was stationed at Sedona, Arizona. This was one of the premier scenic locations in America. I could tell a lot of experiences about that place, but I will confine this story to hunting!

The Sedona District ran from the Mogollion Rim, south of Flagstaff, Arizona, for about 40 miles south descending to high desert country. The most northern part of the district was on the rim. This extremely large plateau is covered by Ponderosa Pine and is probably the largest stand of Ponderosa Pine left in the world.

The actual rim is a huge wall and the road that descends it drops about 3000 feet in a couple of miles. From there on is a deep canyon called Oak Creek Canyon. This canyon runs on down into the high desert country.

Elk and deer are prominent on the upper plateau and are becoming more prominent in the lower areas. At the time I was there, elk had not migrated into the lower country. Deer were scarce in the lower country also and it was difficult to hunt there. I never liked to hunt in timber for deer; however, I have hunted timbered areas for elk for many years.

In 1965 I was attending an in-service training school in New Mexico. Employees were there from several other forests. I was visiting with a ranger from the North Kaibab National Forest. I told him that I didn't have very good hunting on my district. He told me about a 9,000-acre burn that had occurred a few years before, right on the edge of the Grand Canyon, where the Kaibab National Forest met the border of The Grand Canyon National Park. He said deer were plentiful, although the area was a special draw.

I called my brother Charles, who lived in Mesa, Arizona and asked him if he would like to apply and hunt with me. He agreed and was excited about the opportunity. We were successful in getting permits.

The hunt was a late hunt, the beginning of November. The north rim of the Grand Canyon was around 9,000 feet high. I had just purchased a new 1965 Ford Pickup, but it was not 4 x 4, which would cause us some concern later! Pickups with 4 x 4 were just becoming popular and were expensive in those days. Of course, extended cabs and four doors and all of those great options didn't exist at that time.

Charles drove to Sedona and we loaded our gear and were off to the North Kaibab! I had maps and knew about where the burn was located. We didn't have any problems finding the burn, as large as it was. Brush was coming in prominently everywhere, as it does after a major fire. There were a few islands of live trees left, large, over-aged Ponderosa. There were also many large burned snags intermittently throughout the area.

We found a great camping site, just north of the Grand Canyon about a mile. We pulled down into the timber and set up our tent. We didn't have pickup campers or travel trailers or any of those great conveniences. Our tent was about 10 x 10 wall tent. We cooked and performed most of our chores outside the tent.

We arrived the night before the opening day of the hunt. We were excited and had a great time camping. I noticed that high, thin clouds began to appear, boding a possible change in the weather. However, it was warm and pleasant. The area was very rough with narrow ridges, leading down to deep canyons falling off to other large canyons, which in turn, fell off into the main Grand Canyon. A more beautiful, spectacular place could not be found in all of the world!

We decided that we did not want to hunt together. We worked out the areas we would hunt and started on our way. I was shooting my .30-06 that had been purchased in the late 1940's but had been customized by a friend from Idaho.

I started down a long ridge with new growth brush everywhere and a few surviving Ponderosa Pines. I was on a well-traveled deer trail and I soon came upon a few does and they began to work their way ahead of me. Within a mile or so, the number of does had reached 20-25 but not an antler in the group! I kept looking ahead as I quietly stalked down the trail, for a buck. Surely that many does would attract a buck!

But no sign of a buck could be found. Soon I came to a fork in the trail. One fork went down a long ridge north and the other south. I didn't want to follow the trail north so I watched the does disappear into the brush and started south.

The new growth brush began to disappear and I was in an isolated island of Ponderosa pines and large rocks that had not been burned. It was good to feel the pine needles under my feet and I could walk more quietly.

The trail made a sharp turn, near the edge of a canyon to the right. There was a huge rock in front. As I carefully worked my way around this rock, I heard a noise above me. It sounded like animals running in shale or other rock debris. My first thought was that some of the does must not have gone south, but were still ahead of me.

I stepped around the rock and to my surprise two bucks, one very large, in the 26"-30" range and another 18" were moving out ahead of me. I had very little time, but threw up my gun and got off a snap shot at the largest one, which was in the rear. It dropped like a rock. I was delighted. The second deer stopped. Charles and I had an agreement to shoot our own deer. So I watched as it quietly left.

I pumped in another shell and reached down and picked up my empty brass and started up the hill. The shot was about 60 yards. I walked up to where the large buck fell, and to my surprise, not a sign of an animal!

I looked around. Not a drop of blood, not a track, not any sign that an animal had even passed through the area. I looked 50 yards in every direction, but to no avail. Extremely disappointed, I continued south down the trail.

I hunted the general area until noon and stopped to rest in some timber and ate my lunch. I wondered how Charles was doing. I had not seen another person and I had not heard a shot all morning. The thin, high clouds were now much lower and the wind had started to blow. I continued to work my way in the large, planned circle back to camp.

Shortly before sunset the clouds cleared in the far west, just as I stepped out on the main rim of the Grand Canyon. I sat down for a few minutes to think about the day's activities. What an incredible view of the canyon from this angle. As I sat there I wondered if there had ever been another person sit at that place looking west at that angle!

The disappointment of losing the buck didn't seem quite as important at that moment. I stood up and decided I should move rapidly to complete my circle back to camp. Charles returned before I did. He was tired and also disappointed. He had only seen one buck and had not gotten off a shot. His feet were also very sore. We shared the cooking chores and retired to our tent. I had a little portable radio and tuned it to the nearest station, which was Flagstaff, Arizona. The weather report stated that a storm was moving in from the west. I wish that we had cell phones and all of the modern conveniences but we didn't!

The morning dawned much cooler, with a northwest wind and cloudy. We made our plans again and set off. We did not make the same agreement as to shooting each other's deer. (This is called "party hunting." It is illegal, but has been a common practice among hunters for generations. This is especially true for elk hunting, when the primary purpose is to obtain the meat, with little concern for trophies or sport hunting).

I started off in a more westerly direction, hoping to have access to some areas on the map that looked more accessible. However, I soon found box canyons, steep cliffs and difficult areas. I started working my way north and east again as I had the day before. Within an hour I was on the same trail that I had taken yesterday. Only today, there was no sign of any deer. I continued on to where the trail divided. I decided again, not to go north but to work my way south.

I worked my way into the protected, silent island of pines. I came to the rock, and began to work around it. I heard the same animal sounds that I heard the morning before. I looked up and the same two bucks moved out exactly as they had done yesterday! I was much more determined today. I pulled down on the large one, which was last. He dropped again. I pulled down of the smaller one and he dropped.

I did not look down to retrieve my brass. I kept my eye peeled on the little rise and ran up to the largest animal. He was dead, a shot in the neck. The smaller one was also dead, shot behind the shoulder.

I field dressed both of the animals. Then I began to review the actions of both days. I closely examined the large buck. I thought, perhaps, I had hit an antler and knocked him down. Every tine was perfect! I looked for bullet marks everywhere without success. Then I noticed his left, front foot. One half of the hoof was missing! It looked as if it had been neatly cut off with a saw!

It was clear to me now what happened. I shot low, and hit that hoof as he raised it. The impact was enough to knock him down for only a second and he was gone. This happened when I reached down to pick up my brass.

It was about 2:00 when I returned to camp and later when Charles returned. I told him about my morning. He was excited about both animals. We decided we should try to pack them part way out before dark, although we knew we couldn't get them clear to camp.

We had packed them part way out shortly before dark. By now the weather had turned much colder and it was evident that the storm was arriving. I looked around and decided that we should place both animals near a large burned snag, in case it snowed during the night. I was afraid that we could not find them in the brush.

We returned to camp, exhausted. We ate dinner and retired again to our small tent. When we put up the tent, Charles and I had a disagreement on where each of us would sleep. I lost the argument and took the lower area of the tent. About midnight, the rain began to pellet the tent and I slipped deeper in the sleeping bag. About 4:00 a.m., I awoke. My bag felt kind of strange. I turned on the flashlight and looked down. There, at the bottom half of the tent was about four inches of water!

We arose early and looked out. There was about 10 inches of snow on the ground and it was snowing violently! We ate in the tent and tried to protect what gear that had not been put away. By 9:00 a.m., the snow had stopped and there was about 15 inches on the ground. At that elevation, these storms can dump a lot of snow in a short time.

We had walked down the trail a short distance when we came upon another hunter. He was just a kid, standing there with no boots, a light jacket on and distress firmly on his face. He said that he parked his car a few miles down the road and had killed a buck but couldn't take care of it by himself. He had spent the snowy night sitting in his car! We told him that we would be pleased to help him if he would help us get our two animals out first. He agreed and the three of us spent the day packing out three bucks to where we could get them with the truck.

Now the truck was another matter. We broke camp the next morning. The weather was clear and cold. The snow had not melted and probably would not until spring. We turned the truck around and chained it up, hoping to be able to work our way back up to the road. We were successful after an hour or so. I have often thought how useful a 4 x 4 would have been! I have had several pickups since that time…and each one has been a 4 x 4. We loaded the kid's buck in his car, helped him turn around and he followed us out. I don't know what he would have done had he not found us. We often do foolish things when we are young. But in all of my hunting experiences, this has been my only opportunity for a **second chance!**

Over Confidence

I mentioned that I had read about Teddy Roosevelt's hunting experiences on his ranch and on a 10-month safari to Africa. He, like other hunters, learn from their experiences. He went into detail how each animal was shot, how many shots were taken, but always the distance. He developed the habit of continuing to shoot until the animal was down; until the animal was out of sight; or until he ran out of ammunition!

In 1966, I called my brother, Charles and asked him if he would like to go elk hunting with me on the upper part of the Sedona District of the Coconino National Forest. The area was a special limited entry area but not too much competition from other hunters.

He excitingly said yes. He was working on an Arizona Grand Slam. This was a hunting term for successfully killing specific game animals in Arizona. As I recall it included mountain sheep, javelina, mountain lion, mule deer and elk. He had the mountain sheep and the mountain lion but he didn't have the elk. I think that he had more than one mule deer.

We were successful in our license draw. We planned to stay in an old abandoned Forest Service fire lookout cabin, high in the middle of what I thought would be a good elk country. I had used the cabin for camping with my oldest son Mark for father-son outings. It was a nice cabin, old but in good condition. Large enough for several people, with a good heating and cooking stove.

Charles and I arrived the night before the season opened. The weather was warm for November. I never could figure out why the state had such late hunts, especially in the high country. This was an area in the middle of an extremely large Ponderosa Pine plateau. On a clear day, it was easy to stay oriented, but on a cloudy day, it was easy to become confused. On a clear day, the San Francisco peaks, to the north made, a great reference point. I speak from experience on both kinds of days! That reminds me of the story of the old hunter who was once asked if he was ever lost. He replied: "Well, I can't rightly say that I was ever lost, but I have been turned around for several days."

Charles and I had great fun in camping and in brotherly comradeship. We were orphaned when I was five years old. We had very little association after that time. After I moved near him in Arizona, we began to get acquainted with each other. However, I moved away in a few years and I only saw him a couple of more times before he died in 1993.

Neither of us wanted to hunt together. I had been in the country several times and had one particular canyon selected to hunt on opening day. I was going to hunt it myself, but then my conscience started bothering me so I oriented him to that canyon and let him have, what I considered, the best canyon of the whole area.

We each started out in different directions at daylight. At about 9:00 a.m., I heard three shots from that direction and knew that Charles had at least seen something. Our licenses were for bulls only, so I knew that he might have bagged another for his Grand Slam.

I continued to hunt for a few more hours by myself. I returned to the cabin about 4:00 p.m. I walked around the cabin and there he was, leaning on the back of my Ford pickup…a grin on his face. In the bed of the pickup was a very nice, heavy 5 x 5 bull elk. He had retrieved it by himself. It was so large he had to quarter it but he enjoyed the whole operation. Since the weather was warm, we immediately took it to Sedona to a locker plant.

We returned late that night to the cabin. It was difficult driving after dark, but I was fairly familiar with the country. He agreed to stay with me as I hunted for my bull. But I told him I didn't need any help. I was not interested in "Party Hunting." as described above. I hunted all that day without success. A lot of sign but I could not find the elk. Late that night, I awoke to the feared, but not unfamiliar sound of heavy rain on the shingles of that old cabin.

We arose the next morning to a cold, wet rainy day. I watched the temperature, fearing the rain would turn to snow. It did not. In fact it rained all that day and the day after. At the end of the second full day of rain, Charles began to get "cabin fever," and told me that he wanted to go home soon. I asked him to stay one more day for me to hunt. I had not gone out in the rain the two previous days. In those days, Gortex lined boots and all of the rain gear that we have now did not exist. If you were out in the rain, you were wet!

The third day dawned, cloudy and extremely wet, but the rain had stopped, at least for a time. I decided that I would hunt the canyon that Charles had successfully hunted several days before. It was very easy to stalk on a morning like this…a hunter's delight.

I saw some fresh sign in duff of the forest floor and some sign in the mud here and there. I couldn't seem to get any single direction of movement. However, I saw some large tracks and knew they were bulls. I continued to hunt until mid-morning. I knew that Charles would be very anxious to leave, but I could not go back without a strenuous effort to find game.

At about noon, I became somewhat discouraged and started to make a large circle back to the cabin. I had to go through a thick "dog hair" stand of young Ponderosa Pines. I quietly worked back and forth through the pines in an easterly direction. When, suddenly, ahead of me, two 5 x 5 bulls stood up in front of me at about 20 yards. They were each the same size.

I was delighted. I pulled down behind the shoulder of the second one and squeezed off the 150-grain bullet from my .30-06. Then I stood there and waited for it to go down. I watched them both walk ahead of me. But I was so confident that I did not shoot again! So far as I know, they are still walking through the timber! How, I wish that I had the philosophy of Teddy Roosevelt. I have never made that mistake since that time!

I followed their sign but there was not a drop of blood and they were spooked enough that I could not get on them again. After an hour or so, I reluctantly, returned to the cabin. My bullet must have hit one of the saplings that was between me and the elk. I could have easily shot both of them again several times, had I not been so confident of my shooting.

We packed our gear and plowed our way back to Sedona through the mud and small creeks that were over their banks from three days of rain. However, Charles was so pleased that he was one more animal closer towards completing his Grand Slam.

A Missed Geography Lesson

My family and I lived in Bryan, Texas from 1967-1972. I was in graduate school and was teaching at Texas A&M University. Those were very busy days trying to finish school, support a family and remain active in the church. I did have a few opportunities to hunt while living there.

In our department we had an extension division. These men would work on different projects with different people throughout the state...and that was a gigantic state! One extension agent, named Carson Watt was visiting with me one day about one of his projects.

He was working with an owner of a large farm who was converting part of his rice land to catfish farming. He was putting in a series of large ponds, up to 10 acres, as part of his catfish operation. The project was diverse, from raising eggs, to selling brood fish, to offering a pay-as-you-catch sport fishery. I found the project informative, but then real interesting when he mentioned goose and duck hunting on the ponds.

The farm was located about 50 miles east of Houston on the Texas Gulf Coast. This was one of the premier goose and duck hunting areas of the south. The nearby farms had commercial hunting available but this farmer was not into any commercial hunting. Carson asked me if I was interested in going down with him and meeting the manager and, perhaps, hunting while there. I jumped at the chance. We went down one week end. The farmer had just installed a nice new mobile home for guests and we had great accommodations.

The area farmers and hunters had made an agreement to only hunt geese in the mornings and let them rest and settle down each afternoon. There were huge flights of geese and ducks everywhere. The best part of the season was in January. The weather was cool most of the time but occasionally a little warm for hunting. It often rained but that didn't affect the hunting. We would hunt ducks in the afternoon after we finished with the goose hunting. The duck hunting was in the traditional way with blinds on the ponds and using decoys for pass shooting.

I got acquainted with the manager and we became hunting companions when I was there. He was most gracious to me. After meeting him I often went down by myself. At noon, he would show me his market catfish. They were 3-5 pounds, perfect for eating. I would pick one out. He had a cook who would clean and prepare the fish within an hour and we would have lunch. Farm grown catfish is delicious! I prefer a fish with oil and catfish is my favorite…next to King Salmon.

Snow geese were the most common bird in this part of the coast. However, there were greater and lesser Canadas in large flocks. There were many different species of ducks. Mallards seemed to be more prevalent. At least those were the ones most attractive to me for shooting. I spent several week ends down there in the late 1960's.

One particular hunt stands out in my memory. My oldest son Mark was about 10 years old and interested in hunting. That little trooper was always interested in doing things with me when he was young. I had just bought him a little Winchester Model 12, 20-gauge pump shotgun. A very choice gun. (How I wish that I had kept that gun for him but I traded it for a larger gauge gun).

One mistake that I have made in my lifetime is to trade guns. Generally, that is a mistake. I wish that I had kept all of the guns that I have owned. If you want another gun, get it but keep all of them. During the past 40 years, most of the better guns have appreciated in value at probably the same rate as a bank savings account. So why sell them? Some have become very valuable. That Model 12, 20-gauge is now a very valuable gun. Many of the older Browning shotguns have become scarce and are valuable.

Mark wanted to go with me so we went down for a week end together. We had the mobile home to ourselves and had a great time. It is work to prepare for the hunt. We used diapers for decoys! The best place to get them was the diaper service companies that existed in those days. Worn out diapers could be purchased cheap. Each hunter would take a handful and move about the blind or ditch and drop them randomly on the rice stubble. From a distance they looked like snow geese!

Surplus white smocks were acquired for cover for the hunters. We even put the smocks on the black lab retrievers. Two or three hundred diapers in a rice field was a great spread. When a large flock of snow geese becomes committed to landing it is a sight and sound to behold. I have seen geese try to land right next to the dogs wearing the white smocks.

Mark, the manager, and I were out in the middle of this spread for a couple of hours the first morning without success. There were not many geese moving. After a couple of hours we became bored and were about to give up. Mark still had his smock on. It was a little large for him but he didn't complain.

I was looking around and I saw a small flock of geese flying down a fence line to the south of us. I pointed them out to the manager who was a great caller. He gave a honk or two and the geese made one right angle and started north. He gave another series of honks and the geese made another right angle and started west directly toward our decoys. By this time I could see that those birds were Canadas, not Snow Geese and there were nine of them.

I told Mark to quickly lie down and be sure that his smock covered him. The manager and I did the same. When hunting in a spread like this the caller, or one person watches the flock and the other hunters remain hidden, not looking up, for a white face is easily seen by the birds and they will often flare out of range.

The Manager yelled "*Now,*" and I raised up. There they were, in perfect range. I yelled, "Shoot, Mark!" But the little kid was tangled in his smock and couldn't get free in time. I waited a second or two and shot twice as they were going over me. Two Canadas dropped about 40 yards south of us.

Above, Mark with banded Canada geese. Below, hunting with friends on Gulf Coast for geese and ducks, Texas, 1970.

I felt sorry about Mark not getting to shoot but it didn't seem to bother him much. He and I ran out to look at the geese. They were large, greater Canadas. One was a nice sized male. Sometimes when I see a beautiful bird like that, I get a feeling of sorrow for having killed it, but then I remember, with good management, geese and other natural resources are renewable.

We looked over the male closely and behold, there was an aluminum band on one of the legs. I helped Mark remove it and we read the number and the directions to send it to the U.S. Fish & Wildlife Dept. When we returned home, I wrapped it and shipped it off.

We waited and waited. It took about six months for a reply. It was my intention to trace the flight of the bird from where it was banded to Texas and we could have a great geography lesson, with perhaps a few thoughts on how migrations work.

The goose was a 7-year-old male, banded two years before *on a north migration in Oklahoma*. What a disappointment. I was anticipating it being banded in the northern states or Canada, or perhaps even on the distant Hudson Bay. So much for my geography lesson. Mark and I went on to hunt many times in several different states.

The Dancing Buck

I had other responsibilities at Texas A&M University besides teaching and conducting research. One was in counseling students who were majoring in Natural Resource Management. My specialty was in Environmental Interpretation, a discipline closely related to outdoor education, but different in some respects. Although our faculty was diverse, few fished or hunted; most were from urban areas across the nation. Many of the students were from rural Texas and fishing and hunting was very important to them.

Through the years, I became well acquainted with many students from the rural areas of Texas. Most of our undergraduate students were from Texas; many of our graduate students were from everywhere, including several foreign countries. This was one reason the intellectual environment was exciting. While visiting with a student one day, we discussed hunting whitetail deer in Texas. He told me the deer were different sizes, depending upon where they were hunted. I also learned that the population of deer varied greatly across the state. The deer we were talking about were "wild" deer and not those found on game ranches, which were beginning to be developed at that time. Mule deer or black tails were found in west Texas.

Our visit took place in the early part of November, 1970. He mentioned that he would be deer hunting during the Thanksgiving Holiday. He invited me to come and hunt on his Dad's lease, if there was no one else hunting there at that time. I was mildly interested, but cautious about hunting on leases and being too friendly with students.

He dropped by later in the week and told me that the lease was not going to be used and that we were welcome to hunt. I was wondering where we would stay, but before I could ask, he said: "you can stay in our cabin by the creek."

Now the definition of a cabin can vary widely among hunters and fishermen! I have seen some cabins that were practically cardboard boxes. I have seen others that should be called chalets. In my earlier years of hunting, most cabins were tarpaper shacks, especially those buildings on national forests that were built by ranchers to serve as shelters for line riders. I have stayed in several of this type. Sometimes, the more primitive the cabin, the more enjoyable the stay.

I recall one cabin of the chalet type. I had been hunting all afternoon and evening for elk high in the mountains of northeastern Utah near an acquaintance's cabin. This friend had started out hunting below me earlier during the day but had retreated home as soon as the first raindrop fell. This was a "high dollar" cabin, carpeted and with all of the comforts of home. I stayed there one night in the summer and awoke and thought I was in the Radisson Hotel.

Details of that hunt are told in another story titled **Shared Shelter**. I had killed a large bull elk high above his cabin at dark, in the middle of a rain and thunder storm. By the time I had it field dressed and found my four wheeler and finally got to his cabin (his cabin was the nearest to where I was hunting), it was 8:00 p.m. I was bloody, soaking wet, covered with mud and freezing, and needed something hot to drink and eat. I knocked on the door. He and his wife were sitting there when I opened the door and before I could enter they both screamed in unison: *"Don't come in here with those muddy boots."* You just can't worry about muddy boots in a hunting cabin! I fixed something hot to eat and drink when I finally returned to my camping trailer on the other side of the ridge.

But back to my student's invitation. I accepted and we made plans to meet at his home where he would take us to the cabin. I invited my oldest son, Mark who was ten, to join me in this first Texas whitetail hunting adventure.

We arrived on time and he guided us out to the country. Now this cabin was near the San Marcos, Johnson City, Texas area. It was commonly called the Texas hill country. I just drove through there a few weeks ago for the first time since this experience. The hill country is difficult to describe, especially with the canyons and various types of rock outcroppings. It is a great place to live and to hunt.

The student led Mark and me to the cabin over a dusty and primitive road. The cabin had two rooms and a clapboard exterior. It was quite comfortable with a combination wood heating-cooking stove, bunks, table, etc. It was definitely the type of cabin where you wouldn't worry about muddy boots. A clear, bubbling creek ran over limestone outcroppings near the front door.

All around the cabin were scattered groves of various types of oak trees, short and scrubby, typical of the Texas hill country. Mark was immediately drawn to the creek and began its exploration, as any ten-year-old boy would do. In fact, the creek probably remains in his memory more than the deer hunt! It was attractive to me as the water flowed over mottled colored sandstone shelves, creating bowls and rivulets here and there. What a place to play!

It was mid-day and the student told us that he would be back that evening and we would begin our hunt. In the meanwhile he would return to town. I unpacked our gear and laid out the food that we would be having for lunch and dinner that night.

I anxiously awaited his return. I walked the area and began to get a general feeling for the woods and creek. Mark spent the whole afternoon in or near the water. The student returned as promised. He said; "Tonight, I think that we will try a ground blind a couple of miles from here." I had never hunted whitetail but I had read a lot of hunting stories. I knew that most blinds were above ground and some of them were small and very uncomfortable. So this was welcome news to me.

Late in the afternoon, I heard some strange honking sounds from what appeared to be the east. It grew louder. I thought it must be geese, but it didn't sound like geese. It grew extremely loud, even raucous. I ran out of the cabin and looked. Strange birds…then I recognized them. A large flock of Sandhill Cranes. I had never heard them or seen them before. They continued their flight down the creek until they disappeared in the west. In Texas, Sandhill Cranes are considered a waterfowl game bird and are hunted and are eaten…at least they were at that time.

We parked the pickup and began our walk to the blind, Mark trailing behind. I was using my customized .30-06 with a 150-grain bullet. This was my exclusive gun in my earlier years. This caliber, is, in my opinion, the best all-around gun ever made. Of course, I didn't have the money to have more specialized calibers for specific game.

We walked toward a large pile of logs in the middle of a pasture. "Here it is," the student said. I looked. It was just a pile of logs, with brush piled on all sides and a few stumps to sit on. We sat down. Mark tried to sit but had difficulty doing so for more than two minutes. The sun grew low in the west. We were facing east. Our guide told us that the deer could come from any direction and so we should watch everywhere.

In about 30 minutes, due east, I noticed some movements on the edge of the pasture. A doe, no two, now three, now a line of them, perhaps, ten or twelve. They were coming across the pasture at an angle to us. There was little or no wind. They all looked like does. No antler in sight. By the time they were across from us, in easy range, I spotted the buck.

He was coming much slower, head down and occasionally stopping and smelling and then putting his nose into the air. He could easily see the does ahead of him but this was normal behavior in the rut. I said: "Mark, watch, here comes a buck." Mark immediately found a peep hole in the pile of logs and watched the buck's movements.

The buck was coming across at exactly the same angle after the does. The does disappeared behind us but the buck continued on in his steady but moderate pace. I wondered when to shoot, or should I shoot. He didn't look very big. He would be considered a "basket buck" in Kansas.

When he was about a hundred yards to my left he stopped. I clicked off my safety and slowly placed the gun across a log at the most comfortable height. Mark was now right at my side watching intently. Our host made no sounds or suggestions. All of a sudden the buck stopped and looked in all directions. He must have smelled us. Then, to my *astonishment*, he stood high on his hind legs and made a complete circle, looking for the source of our scent. He dropped down, apparently more agitated than before. Mark said: "Shoot him, Dad, shoot him!" I placed the cross hair slightly behind his shoulder and squeezed it off. The buck would never dance again.

Mark and the author with the "dancing buck," Texas, 1970.

We ran over to see the antlers. I looked down. He was so small. It was now I realized that the more prevalent the deer in Texas, the smaller the size, which is not the case in other places. We field dressed the deer and carried it to the pickup. It weighed about 70 pounds, a good average deer for that part of Texas.

Our host took care of the deer and we returned to the cabin. It had a welcome look. Serious hunting cabins will have a welcome look when you return to them. Mark and I had dinner and crawled into our bunks. As I reviewed the evening's activities, I realized the hunt was over already and we would be going home tomorrow. I thought of Mark and said: "What did you think of the dancing buck?" but he was asleep

Real Guides Don't Smoke

During the early spring of 1994, during a day of extreme boredom at work, I was reviewing some literature from different guides and outfitters who specialized in elk and deer hunting. The various types of literature were glowing in descriptive terms with impressive kill-ratio statistics. That evening, in a moment of weakness, I called the one that looked most impressive.

Now, it should be remembered, that, in my opinion, there are more crooks, liars and exaggerators in this business, than any other that I know. This is about the only purchase that has to be made in advance, with no return policy, no guarantees and no recourse, if dissatisfied. But that didn't stop me from booking a hunt for late November with an outfitter by the name of Andy Sidewinder. This was in the north-central part of Montana, out of White Sulphur Springs, on a 45,000-acre private lease. Now, I didn't want to go by myself, so I immediately called my friend Robert Ruude, or "Fat Bob," known to those who dare call him that, primarily me. He was very hesitant and that should have been fair warning to me, but I persisted.

This hunt was for elk and deer. Montana is another in a large number of states that are so corrupt that they require you to buy both licenses, even though you only intend to hunt one or the other. The policy is for non-residents only. My priority was for elk, although, according to our guide, getting both would be "no problem." The plans were made, deposits sent and we waited for November to arrive.

Our accommodations were arranged at White Sulphur Springs in the middle of the vast, rolling, pine-covered hills of north central Montana. Fat Bob and I were to share a very nice room in a large bed and breakfast home. We were the only guests since this was the late hunt and there were no tourists. Another reason may have been because there was a foot of snow on the ground and the temperature was about 10 degrees during the day. That didn't bother me...I like to track elk in the snow. Of course I was not as young as I used to be.

We arrived in mid-afternoon and were graciously greeted and shown to our room. The hosts of the B&B had a permanent arrangement with the guide. Andy Sidewinder had the lease for part of the large ranch. The ranch was divided into two parts the other part was even larger with 50,000 acres.

He apparently had more than one party hunting but the ranch was huge and diverse and there would be little competition. He owned nothing but a couple of pickups. Andy, himself, would be our personal guide.

Andy said that he would pick us up at promptly 5:00 a.m. and to be ready, he didn't like to wait. We were up, breakfast eaten and anxious for our first day of a six-day hunt. It was cold. We kept our guns and snow gear out in a porch. When I picked up my gun, I thought it might freeze to my hand.

We had driven to Montana in my new 1994 4 x 4 propane powered, roomy, extended cab pickup. I thought of it as I was crammed into a small, standard cab, late 1970 vintage 4 x 4 Chevy pickup. Now, we all had to sit in the single seat. The guide was big, Fat Bob was bigger and I was forced to ride on the door handle.

We started off and, within 30 seconds, out came a cigarette, and the smoke permeated the small air space. I said: "I'm allergic to cigarette smoke and would appreciate you not smoking in the pickup." He acted as if he didn't hear me.

Now the game plan for the first day was to intersect large herds of elk as they return from the lower pastures early in the morning to their cover areas high in the pine covered rolling hills. Sounds good to me, I've done that before! Apparently, Andy had been using this system for all of the other parties that preceded us, with relatively good luck.

Several bulls were killed, some with impressive racks. We saw several herds, sneaked up to within shooting range...but no bulls. Lots of cows. By 11:00, the guide said: "let's go back to town." I didn't know why. He pulled into our B&B and said, "I'll pick you up about 4:00 p.m. and we'll try it again." I looked at Fat Bob and then at him and said: "What are we supposed to do all day?" Andy didn't bother to answer and was gone in a minute. (Later, I was to find out that he spent the day in town, on personal business, most of which was conducted at the local bar). We went inside, had lunch and I told Fat Bob that I did not intend to spend my days in town when I came here to hunt.

Andy returned as arranged. We waited for the elk to come down that night but we never saw any. He took us back after dark. As I was getting out I told him to have lunch for the next day and that I intended to spend a full day hunting. I also told him I could get out and walk, in case he had never heard of that activity while hunting. Fat Bob did not enter into any of our discussions.

The next day: 5:30; same scene, same temperature, same snow and the same cigarette. I had breathed so much second hand smoke that I was thinking about taking up the habit again myself. We spotted a large herd of elk ambling their way along a ridge with heavy cover along one side. There was also a fence running west and south. We would have to make a long stalk...good; no more cigarette smoke.

We stopped to rest in a draw. Our plan was to slowly top the hill. The elk should be in range from that point. I was heavily dressed, with several layers. The guide looked at me and said: "You make too much noise stalking. Have you ever hunted before?" This surprised me as he took out a cigarette and lit it. I watched the smoke curl toward the direction of the elk. I responded by saying: **"Real guides don't smoke."**

As we topped the hill Fat Bob decided to go left around a grove of pines. Nimrod Andy and I were to go straight. There they were, about sixty of them. Where were the bulls? Suddenly I saw two rag horn bulls (very small 4 x 4s and 5 x 5s). They were all milling at about 100 yards toward the corner where the two fences joined. They were running side by side directly away. I shot twice but missed. I watched the bulls jump the fence and all of the cows but one calf jump the fence. It ran back and forth and then finally got courage and jumped and joined the rest of the herd as it ran out of sight. Fat Bob had also shot two or three times. The guide was pretty miffed and this began the first of some derogatory and vulgar language directed towards me.

We walked toward the corner of the fence. We topped a little rise and there at the foot of it was a dead cow elk. Now, Andy was really angry. Fat Bob and I began to discuss who shot it. I didn't think that I did and told him so but said: "I *might* have shot it." Cow season would open the next day so we could keep it. The guide said he would call the warden and tell him what happened. Fat Bob agreed to tag the cow. That meant that I could still hunt a bull.

I honestly don't know if I shot the cow or not. However, this issue and some other disagreements have ruined our relationship. Fat Bob began to be sullen and very abusive to me. Fat Bob had retired out of the Army as a colonel and had a hard time realizing that he was no longer in charge of all those around him. Andy continued to smoke and I began to regret the whole experience. Fat Bob later retrieved the bullet from the cow and insists that it was from my gun. But by now, who cares?

I reviewed the situation that night as I went to bed: The bulls are gone from the herds; the rut is over and they are hiding in the canyons and other areas. I resolved that I was not going to spend another four days using this futile method of hunting. I knew what I would do.

The next day I told the Andy that I wanted to "spot and stalk." which is the standard method of hunting. If there is nothing to spot, then I want to walk the canyons on foot. He said he didn't want to hunt this way. Fat Bob would not support me. He was fat and out of shape and was not interested in walking very far. In fact he spent most of the hunting trip sitting in the cab of that old truck.

Later in the morning we spotted a small herd with one bull, with a deformed antler on one side. It would make a good trophy. The elk slowly grazed toward a draw and laid down. However, I could see the antlers of the bull sticking up and I knew right where he was. I said I can slip over there and catch him, under cover, from the west and he will never see me. We argued about it until the bull moved and it was too late.

I insisted that we walk and begin to work the canyons. The guide realized that I was getting angry and agreed. We stalked several canyons and saw elk but no bulls. That evening shortly before dark, we came across some fresh tracks going up a ridge into cover. I got out and started to track them; Andy reluctantly joined me. Fat Bob dozed in the truck.

The wind was blowing in our face as we climbed the steep hill. The snow was drifting and it was well above my knees as we continued to climb the hill. I told the guide that the elk should be on the lee side of the hill and we could easily get up on them. He didn't say anything but just followed. In a few minutes we heard a loud bull bugle below us in the timber. We then went across the ridge into the wind.

Instead of being on the lee side, the cows were grazing and the calves actually cavorting in the snow banks on the windward side of that hill. I couldn't believe it. We dropped into the snow. There were cows and calves within 30-50 feet of us but the wind and snow were blowing so hard they never detected us. I said: "let's wait, the bull will come up from below and we can get a shot at him." The cows and calves moved back and forth but never did see us. Within a few minutes it was too dark to shoot and we turned and worked our way down the hill to the truck.

I knew now that we could find elk and we could find bulls. We just had to get out of that pickup and hunt. But each following day was the same. The guide smoked and cussed, Fat Bob pouted and continued to be unpleasant. He remained in this mood through the evening. He was even worse in the morning before he had his coffee. One morning, we had a serious altercation, but his behavior did not change.

Andy met us the last day. He seemed to be in a better mood. One more day and we would be gone and he would have another group, the last of the year coming to hunt. We drove around for the morning. We went to town and took care of the cow. It was noon. Time was running out. I told him I wanted to hunt a specific canyon that we had hunted earlier in the week. He said: "No, but I will take you to another canyon to hunt." I knew that he was playing for time and it angered me.

Elk hunting had been so difficult that we only spent one day on deer and could not get within shooting range of any in some lower pastures of the ranch. I had a sandwich and Andy had a cigarette. We drove up this canyon. It was now about 2:00 p.m. We spotted several deer. One large buck was resting on a ridge about 150 yards above us. Fat Bob didn't say anything to me, he just got out and shot it. It was a good shot and a nice 5 x 5 buck. We put it in the truck and continued on. I looked high on a ridge to the left and spotted elk grazing. Andy stopped the truck. I told him I was going to stalk them, with or without him. He said he would go with me but we would try to intersect them from a different angle. I had no objection to this. Off he went as hard as he could go, with me trying to keep up with him in the deep snow.

The ridge was steep, the snow deep and I was 62 years old! I asked him to slow down as I fell behind him. I decided that he would not let me get out of sight, so I slowed down. He slowed down. Soon, it became evident to me that we were not tracking the elk that we originally saw. I caught up with him and told him. He acknowledged it and told me that we were trailing another herd and they were going toward a canyon that he knew well.

I was getting extremely tired. We topped a ridge. Andy took his binoculars and glassed the area below. At about 500 yards, there were several cows in an opening. He couldn't see a bull. While he looked, I caught my breath. Then, he said: "A bull just got up and is in the opening." I took the binoculars and looked. It looked like a small 5 x 5. It began to move slowly around the opening.

By now my dislike for this guy was intense! Andy said: "Shoot him." I responded that I had never shot an animal at over 500 yards in my life. I then started to go down toward the elk. The wind was in our favor. I could get closer. He said: "Shoot him here and now." I stopped and thought: "This is the last day, it will be dark in 30 minutes, there will not be another chance. I might as well try."

There was a log in a snowdrift right on the crest of the ridge. It was a long ways down that draw. I put my hands in my pocket. I counted nine shells. I decided that I would shoot nine times until the animal was down or gone. I dropped into a prone position in the snow across the log. The snow was blowing in my face. I was angry. Down hill, at least 500 yards and windy. What is the trajectory drop of a .30-06? The bull was now broadside, facing east. I placed the crosshair right on the top of his shoulder. I squeezed it off. Andy was watching in his binoculars. "You missed the son-**-*-****." I crammed another 165-grain bullet into the chamber. The crosshair was right on the shoulder and I squeezed it off again. "You missed again. You can't hit anything." The bull disappeared. I was extremely disappointed.

Andy looked at me with disgust. But I gazed down into the meadow and the bull was walking back into the open! All of the cows were gone. He went into the middle of the opening and laid down, facing the opposite direction, into the wind.

I said: "the bull's hit hard and he is lying down." We stood on the log to look below. "Shoot him again," said the guide. I didn't respond, I just started down the long ridge. The wind and snow were blowing directly in my face so I knew the elk could not hear me. Some of the drifts were three and four feet deep. I tried to avoid them as I slipped over some minor ledges.

Above, more than two shots in the vital area were needed to down this 4 x 4 elk. Below, the same bull elk bagged in spite of an incompetent outfitter, Montana, 1994.

I got to within 100 yards of him, with no cover between us. The bull continued to look directly west toward the nearest timber. What I should I do? There was nothing to use for a rest. I waited a couple of minutes and tried an off-hand shot, toward the center of the back of his neck. A second after the shot rang out, the elk was up and running toward the timber and then disappeared.

By now, Andy had caught up with me. He was livid with anger and was cursing and carrying on. He said: "Now you've lost him for good." I retorted: "He was fatally hit and we could find him tonight or in the morning." The guide hissed: "I have other hunters coming in tonight."

He reached for my gun and said: "I'll take care of that elk." I said: "You will like Hell," pulled away and started to track the elk into the timber. The light was almost gone as I entered the timber. I walked for about 50 yards and spotted the elk with his head down, obviously mortally wounded. A rapid shot through the neck finished him.

I let the guide field dress the bull, which was a large 4 x 4. His body was larger than the antlers would indicate. We then laboriously moved the elk over downed logs to the edge of the timber. It was now totally dark. There was about 16 inches of snow on the ground. As I moved around, I kept barking my shins on buried logs and rocks.

The truck was about two or three miles from this spot. It was getting colder. Andy lit a cigarette and said: "Let's get going." I told him that we should wait for the full moon to come up in just a few minutes and we could easily see our way back to the truck. He apparently was tired of arguing with me. The moon soon arose and reflected off the snow. We could easily see to move around. By now the temperature had dropped to about 0 degrees. But I had a warm glow as we started up the ridge to return to the truck.

It was a beautiful night for walking. I wanted to enjoy it so I dropped a hundred yards behind my companion and stayed there until we found our pickup. Fat Bob was distressed. He said: "Where the Hell have you guys been?" He wasn't satisfied, even after I told him about the afternoon's activities.

Andy said that we had to get the bull out tonight. It was okay with me but Fat Bob wasn't very enthused. We chained all four wheels of the truck and started a long circle to find the elk. It was a tough ride but we finally backed to within a few yards of the elk. The truck had a small electric winch on the bed and we pulled the big bull into the truck with very little effort. There was not much said on the way to town. Fat Bob was mad. Andy had missed his appointment with his new hunting party and I was exhausted.

After we returned to the B&B we backed right up to my pickup and four of us transferred the elk. Andy said nothing as he climbed into his truck and roared away. I was disappointed. I thought Fat Bob would want to give him a tip! By now it was 11:00 p.m. We went inside and quickly went to bed.

The next morning dawned bright and cold. We packed our gear. We then retrieved the cow elk from the locker plant and headed for Kansas. The three animals made a significant load for our truck.

The day and a half ride back to Kansas wasn't very pleasant. The relationship between Fat Bob and me appeared to be over. I was not disappointed. We had been on several trips, including two to Alaska. But he had become increasingly unpleasant. I could find another, more compatible hunting companion.

After returning to Kansas, I examined the bull elk. It had two shots behind the shoulder, four inches apart. It also had a sharp cut, made by a bullet across one side of the neck. My first question was why didn't two shots in the vital area put the elk down sooner? It appeared that the distance was so great that the impact was significantly reduced. I have shot many animals successfully in the vital area, but never at such a distance. As I reviewed that hunt, I was hopeful, for the benefit of the next hunters, that Andy would run out of cigarettes!

Hunting the Wind River Range

In 1956, I became acquainted with several men in Casper who liked to hunt. One of them, Ivan Allred, told me of a ranch that we could hunt elk out of if we could get a special permit, since it was a limited entry area. We both applied and we were both successful.

Ivan introduced me to the ranch hand and his family who lived at the headquarters on the Wind River, four miles west of Dubois, Wyoming. Ivan and I hunted there one year. He never returned but I became friends with Bob and Meg Lucas and returned many times.

The operation of this ranch was very difficult and profits were few. It was managed as a cow-calf operation, including growing native hay on the pastures where possible. Bob was in charge of most of the operation with seasonal hands to assist him.

The ranch buildings were located on the edge of the river. The bridge across the river belonged to the ranch and access was controlled. The bench across and above the ranch was private land and the Shoshone National Forest surrounded the entire area. Bob could lock the gate and he could control the hunters entering at that location. This was a great advantage to have such hunting privileges. Although access to the area was possible from the east and west, it was very difficult and other hunters were seldom seen in the general area.

Things have changed. As I now drive through the area, it is hard to imagine how it used to be! The ranch is gone. A modern bridge is now located where that old sagging wood bridge used to be. The bench is now subdivided and there are many expensive homes located there.

It was a delight for me to hunt out of that ranch. This was an original working ranch with several buildings. The main ranch house was small, with a couple of bedrooms. I stayed in what was originally the bunkhouse for ranch hands. It was in a decaying stage but I didn't mind sharing the room with mice and other rodents. I slept on an old sagging bunk bed. Surrounding the house were all of the other usual barns and outbuildings.

Through an 8-10 year period, I was successful in drawing a permit every year for elk of either sex. The area was an open area for deer of either sex. I was seldom interested in a female deer but elk are so difficult and the meat so superior that we often killed cows.

The following accounts stand out in my mind as the more interesting of the many times that I have hunted there. The stories are not necessarily in chronological order.

Cow Elk Have Long Necks

Cow elk and bull elk probably have about the same neck length, but bulls have antlers, sometimes large and impressive. This gives them a balanced look. In my opinion, a mature bull elk is one of the most beautiful animals that exist. Cow elk look gangly and when they run they appear ungainly and out of balance. This does not mean they cannot run fast; they are incredibly strong and intelligent. They have an uncanny sense of hearing, smell and sight. In a way they look like camels. A camel, to me, looks as if it was designed by a committee.

In 1956, I purchased a 1941 Ford Pickup. I paid $250 for it. At the time I was making $1.30/hour as an apprentice printer. I needed something to hunt in. Cars are not effective vehicles for hunting, although I had used them many times. Four wheel drives (4 x 4), did not exist in those days, except for Army surplus Jeeps and Dodge Power Wagons. The first new 4 x 4 truck available, in the early 1950s, was a small Jeep pickup. They had an undersized 4-cylinder engine. The bed was very small and the cab was even smaller. However, with the front wheel drive and several gear options, they could go where no other truck could go.

A friend, Ivan Allred, had met Bob Lucas, the rancher mentioned above the year previously. Ivan and I received our limited entry permit for the area above the ranch. However, another friend of Ivan's, Lavelle Peterson, wanted to hunt elk on the general open area in the Jackson Hole, Wyoming area. This was, perhaps, the most famous area in America, to hunt elk. I had the pickup, which may have been the reason that I was invited to go with them.

We spent four days trying to find an elk. I do not remember even finding a track! We didn't know where the better hunting areas were and we were really novices. I had only hunted elk once with Dave, in the late 1940's. This was in the same general area but I could not remember the location. After four days of camping out, Lavelle had to return home. As I recall, he had left his car someplace between Jackson Hole and Casper.

He returned and Ivan and I decided to stop in the Wind River Range and use our special permits.

As a side comment…this was the only time I hunted with Lavelle. Several years later, after I had left Casper, he was involved in a tragic accident where his hunting partner was accidentally shot and killed during an elk hunt. In my years of hunting, I have had a couple of near misses, but this is the only example of a lethal accident.

We pulled into the ranch about noon. Ivan introduced me to Bob and Meg Lucas. They were a young couple about our ages, with two little boys in diapers. It was a tough life in those times for them. However, they were kind, friendly and hospitable to us as strangers.

After visiting and getting general directions, Ivan and I decided that we would hunt that afternoon. It was about seven or eight miles up from the ranch to where we were going to hunt. Traveling that road was slow and laborious. The Ford was beginning to make some strange sounds in the rear differential. It was a manual 4-speed and powerful enough. I worked my way through the bogs, wet spots, a few snow banks, and washouts until we found ourselves high above the ranch. We parked along some granite outcroppings with a gorgeous view of the whole area to the north. We could see for 50 miles in every direction.

I looked south from where the road ended. There were a series of breaks and canyons leading higher to timber line. It was a mile or more before there was any cover. I looked at Ivan and said: "I sense there are some elk in this area; *I feel it!*" He asked me where I was going to hunt. I told him I was going over to the nearest breaks and then climb a few ridges and make a circle back to the truck by dark. This was an ambitious hike, but in those days I could hike, seemingly, forever.

Ivan had been dozing as we made our climb up the mountain. He looked at me and said he would "watch for elk from the truck." I looked around the area and thought "you could wait on this sidehill for a lifetime and never see an elk." I said: "Do you want me to shoot your elk?" Remember, we were meat hunting as well as being hopeful of finding a bull. He said: "No, I'll take care of my own."

It was a beautiful fall afternoon, in mid-September. The sky was cloudless. I had a snack, put on a jacket and looked south. It had snowed a few days before. Most of the snow was gone in the sun-exposed areas. But on the north slopes and in the shady spots there were a few inches of melting snow.

I walked briskly south until I entered the first of the scattered timbered draws. I looked down and there was a beautiful set of what appeared to be fresh bear tracks. (In those days, elk and deer licenses included a bear tag). The bear was going in the same direction that I wanted to go, so I carefully followed the wandering tracks around trees and rocks and bushes, but still in a southerly direction. I kept looking ahead, hoping to see the bear. This went on for 20 minutes. All of a sudden, the tracks make a sharp turn to the right and went west. I thought about following them further but that was not in the direction I wanted to go. I must make a circle to be back by dark.

I turned and began a southeasterly direction along a ridge. Then, I dropped off the ridge into a beautiful hidden valley area. The trees were old growth firs and spruce. Moss was on the ground and on decaying logs from trees long since fallen. The snow was not melting here. I quietly worked my way to the bottom, slipping here and there on soaked branches hidden in the snow.

I glanced to my left and there were fresh elk tracks. They looked really fresh, with a pile of steaming dung! They were fresh tracks! I walked another hundred yards, looked to my left and saw a cow elk curled up next to a log. I looked behind her and there were several cows and calves standing quietly. I looked for a bull. None. I counted them, eight that I could see. They had not detected my presence and I was within forty yards of them.

Which one should I shoot? I became nervous, not knowing what to do. I kneeled down. I removed my safety off my Model 70, .30-06. It made a "click." Upon hearing this, the cow asleep by the log raised its head and stretched its neck as far as it would go. It looked like a camel. The elk looked right at me but I did not move. It rolled its ears in a strange circle. It turned to look to the right. I placed the crosshair directly in the center of the neck and squeezed off a shot.

Its head dropped and it never moved an inch. The other elk saw me now and one by one walked by me at 30 yards. I thought about Ivan's remark: "No, I'll take care of my own." So I watched each one parade slowly by me.

I walked up to the elk, placed my gun on the log, pulled my knife out of the sheath. I looked at the hole in the neck, with a small trickle of blood showing on the bottom side. I thought that I would place the knife in the hole to finish cutting the throat to speed up the bleeding process. When my knife was about six inches from the neck, all of a sudden, a loud snort came from the cow, up she jumped, and knocked me backward. My knife flew into the air and disappeared!

In a second, she was running and gone. My heart pumped wildly, as I kneeled in the snow covered moss. What should I do now? In a couple of minutes, I regained my composure. She could have killed me! (I won't go into detail about what I learned from this experience, but I never made that mistake again).

I looked at my gun. It was not disturbed. Then I remembered my knife. I looked for several minutes before I found it in the snow. I stood up, still shaken by the experience. I picked up my rifle and began to track the elk.

Within a few feet, I could see blood covering the tracks. It looked as if it had been sprayed. I now knew what had happened. The shot was in the center of the neck, but below the spine. The mane made the neck appear thicker and the shot was low. It had apparently nicked both the jugular vein and the windpipe, thus causing the spraying effect.

I felt confident that I could track the elk down. The tracks went south for a distance and then west, up the ridge, moving away from the truck. I walked briskly, following the tracks. I looked and sighted her yellow rump as she worked her way upward. I thought that wounded animals went downhill! I couldn't get a shot. She kept going until she came to a rock ledge with a 20 foot drop below. I found her hidden behind a huge boulder, mortally wounded. I quickly shot her, in case she should continue away from the truck. I was aware of the work that it would take to transport the meat back to the truck.

My first elk. What a difficult and dangerous experience. I was embarrassed, but thankful for finding the small herd. Had I shot a bull the same way, I could have been gored. Elk are large animals. I realized this as I field dressed her. It took over an hour to finish. I spread her rib cage with a branch so she would cool during the night. I looked around for landmarks so that I could find her in the morning. Then I started my long trek back to Ivan and truck.

I arrived an hour before dark. Ivan looked as if he had napped all afternoon. He was pleased, but at first unbelieving that I could track and kill an elk so "easily" as he put it. I didn't go into details about the experience beyond finding the herd. As a matter of fact, I have never mentioned this experience, except to illustrate the need for clean kills and caution as a downed animal is approached.

The next morning we returned from the ranch and worked our way as near as possible to the trail to the downed elk. What a difference a 4-wheeler would have made! However, it would be decades before these incredible machines would be available to sportsmen. We each carried a quarter out at a time. Exhausting work. It took most of the day. Bob looked at our elk and was pleased for our success. Ivan didn't want to hunt any more. He claimed that half of the elk was his for having carried it out. I didn't object, but I knew that we could have had double the meat!

I told Bob that I would be back next year and that I appreciated his hospitality. Indeed, I went back many times. I never hunted with Ivan again. I don't think he ever hunted elk again, at least not from that ranch. I found out what the strange noise coming from the rear end of the pickup was. After returning home, I parked the truck in front of the house. It groaned once and the whole rear end was gone! I sold it exactly as it sat for $200. I have never had good experiences with Fords. It all started with that pickup.

Machine-Gun Kelly

Game and fish rules and regulations have changed a lot over the years. All government agencies become increasingly stringent and prohibitive. These changes and new restrictions are always touted as "advantages for the sportsmen." In the 1950s, residents and ranchers could guide non-residents and others on private and public lands, where now there are restrictive rules and regulations.

Bob Lucas was always trying to generate extra money on the ranch above his meager salary. One way was to guide non-residents in hunting elk and deer on the Shoshone National forest.

Those years, I was an apprentice printer, working on the *Casper Morning Star*. This was a morning paper. I finished my shift about 1:00 a.m. I usually went home, packed and headed for Dubois. I could arrive on opening morning of the elk and deer season. I seldom hunted deer there. I usually hunted deer nearer to Casper. But I was always anxious to hunt elk out of that ranch.

I arrived one year to find that my bunkhouse had two other hunters from Michigan sleeping there. Bob was sort of helping them hunt deer and elk. Those men were not strangers to me. We had all been together the year before.

The year before, Bob had asked me to help "orient" the hunters to some of the better canyons. Normally, I only hunt alone. By that I mean, I want to hunt and stalk by myself. Often, I will be around other hunters but we will hunting by ourselves, meeting once or twice a day where possible.

I told Bob that I would take one of them up to one of my favorite areas and direct him "where to go" but not accompany him. They both agreed to this arrangement. The hunter seemed pleasant enough. We visited as we walked down the trails. This whole area had been logged in the early 1930s and many of the skid trails and access roads were still usable.

We were briskly walking down one of those trails. I looked ahead and spotted a bull moose, broadside, grazing at about a hundred yards. I said: "Look at that moose ahead on the trail." The hunter said: "Where?" But before, I could respond, up came his .300 Winchester Magnum and the moose was down!

I couldn't believe this had happened. There were a lot of moose around the general area but there were no moose permits available. I said: "Why did you do that?" He never answered. In fact he was asked that question by his hunting partner, Bob Lucas and me at least three times. He never did answer the question.

I didn't know what to do. I looked at that magnificent animal, well shot, but under threat of being totally wasted. The antlers were small, with a 5-inch palm. It would be very good eating. I told the hunter to help me field dress it. We spread its rib cage and pulled it into the timber and hid it as best you can hide an 1100 pound animal. I was anxious to get away from this guy. I pointed out where he should go and then went my own way.

Late that afternoon, I killed a nice cow standing on an old sawdust pile. The piles were slowly deteriorating and this process caused heating. Many animals like to stand or lie on them in the cold weather. The snow always melts first on the piles. Some of them were very large. They were created by portable sawmills that were common when those areas were cut over.

I worried all day about telling Bob about the moose problem. Poaching an elk is one thing. There were plenty of them, but not a moose. We were all hopeful that they would reproduce to the point where we could have an open season, or at least a limited entry system. This never happened while I was in Wyoming and I doubt that it has happened since that time.

The hunter returned to the ranch before I, but had not told anyone about the moose. I went to the kitchen of the ranch and visited with Bob and Meg. In my exasperation about the whole ordeal, I said: "Bob, how could you send me out with **Machine-Gun Kelly?** That was the name of a famous criminal during Al Capone's days. He used a machine gun to mow down other gang members. This would be the hunter's name for as long as I knew him or ever referred to those experiences.

Bob and I decided that we would not waste the meat. He and I drove up the mountain the next day and retrieved both animals. I left the following day. As I went through the Game and Fish Check Station, out of Dubois, I was probably the only hunter with an elk that had five quarters.

The Bugling Bulls

The next year, when I realized that Machine-Gun Kelley (MGK) was back, I knew that Bob would probably want to use me in some manner. I didn't know what to say when the request came again. Bob said: "Just take him up to some of the areas again and let him go." I agreed. Bob said that he would take the other hunter east, about four miles from where we would be hunting. Bob showed me a new bull bugle that he had made out of a piece of plastic pipe. It sounded pretty good.

We all started out together in an old Jeep pickup of the type discussed above. The pickup smoked, burped and put a blue haze into the air. MGH and I got out together and the other two hunters drove east to where they would hunt. Bob told me to try to be at a well known ridge by 1:00 p.m., if possible. I agreed, but I did not intend to be there with MGH!

As we wound our way up and down the trails, I watched very carefully for moose or elk or any other animal that might be seen. Fortunately, no animals were seen before I pointed out the route I suggest that he take for the day's hunt.

It was still very early but the light was good. I started at the base of a long meadow, stretching up a half mile alongside of a ridge. I glanced up the meadow to the top. There was an animal grazing about half way up, near an isolated group of firs. I threw up my scope. It looked like it might be a large buck deer. I could make out the antlers from that distance.

I made a mental note of a huge snag on the edge that would guide me to the location. I stepped out of the meadow and started up the timbered ridge at a near run. I didn't go far until I realized how steep it was and how hard I was breathing. I was also tired from working my night shift and having no sleep. I slowed my pace. I kept looking for the snag to guide me to the buck. I slipped out to the edge of the timber, but at that angle I couldn't see up the meadow.

Soon, I spotted the snag. I kneeled at the base and rested until I felt that I had my composure. I slowly crawled forward and looked west to where I thought the buck should be. A perfect plan. There he was, at about 80 yards, grazing with his head in the opposite direction. I waited until he turned and looked closely at his antlers. A nice 5 x 5, perhaps 28 inches wide.

Plenty good. Should I take him? If I take my deer on this trip, I will not be able to hunt again in the low country, in October. I couldn't resist. I used no rest. I stood, and shot off-hand. One shot, down he went. My 150-grain .30-06 bullet through the lower part of his neck. In those days, I used 150 grains for most all game. I tried the 180 grain and even the 220 grain, but found both too heavy. Now, I use 165 grains, which I think is the best weight.

I field dressed the buck and pulled him into the shade. I have never been very fast at field dressing. When I hurry, I usually cut my hands on sharp bones. It took me about an hour. I knew now, that I would never be to the appointed ridge on time. But it didn't matter. Bob would not be upset. He would have known that something delayed me.

I continued up the long meadow. It was easier hiking than through the timber. At this elevation there was a lot of windfall and very difficult to walk through. These areas will exhaust hunters very soon. I worked my way to timberline. What a great area. What a view! For years I would walk the same trails and make the same circles back to the truck. I was working my way east, right at timberline. Large boulders were randomly scattered through the area.

The grass and late blooming flowers softened the sound as I went along. I was extremely tired. I was feeling the effects of the elevation, heavy exertion and lack of sleep. I sat at the base of a boulder and rested.

I rested for 10 minutes, got up and began a long slow walk along the ridge running east. I began to feel worse, a little sick to my stomach. I knew that the elevation and exertion were bothering me. What should I do? It was about the same distance either way back to the truck. I elected to go on, and make the circle. I glanced ahead and thought that I saw an animal move into the timber. I couldn't be sure. I looked for some kind of a landmark to mark the location.

As I neared the area where I thought I saw the animal, I looked for tracks…nothing. I moved closer to the timber and began looking down into the timber. The trees were old growth, spruce and firs. This was a virgin area. No cutting had been done at this elevation. I saw nothing and continued. Just before the crest of the ridge, a faint trail went into the timber. I followed it for about 50 feet.

I was startled. Directly in front of me at 20 yards, in clear view, was a 5 x 5 bull elk, looking intently down into the timber. An incredibly easy shot. At that distance, the impact was devastating. One shot behind the shoulder knocked it completely off its feet. It never took a step.

I forgot about my elevation sickness. He was so large that I had a difficult time turning him over on his back to dress him. I usually pull the antlers back and stick them into the ground to stabilize the body for field dressing. Then, I place a log or large rocks along each side to keep it from rolling over. The hill was steep but I finally managed to finish the job. Seldom can a hunter bag a 5 x 5 deer and a 5 x 5 elk in one morning. I was so pleased and thankful.

When I finished, I became sick to my stomach again. I ate some jerky, a candy bar and drank a few sips of water. I slipped down and laid back on the elk. How should I go back? The shortest route is not always best if you are not feeling well. I elected to take a little longer route but with easier trails.

By the time I returned to the ranch late that afternoon, I was feeling much better. The others had all returned but none had the opportunity for a shot at a deer or an elk. I told my stories to MGK, his partner and to Bob. The Michigan hunters appeared angry that I had been so successful. MGK's partner said that I probably killed his elk!

Then Bob told me *his* story. They had hunted most of the morning without success. At about the time that I was high on the ridge, they heard a bugle. Bob began to bugle back. Soon there were two bulls answering his calls. However, they could never get either bull to come in. Then they said they heard a shot high on the ridge. It was my shot. Apparently the bull I shot was listening intently to the other bulls bugle. That was the reason I could slip up on him so easily!

The next day dawned cold and windy. A storm might be on the way. Bob and I put Whitey, his old white work horse into the horse trailer and laboriously worked our way up the mountain. By the end of the day we had both animals safely home. The elk was quartered but we brought the buck deer back whole. I always enjoy the animals more when whole than after they are quartered. While whole they are trophies; quartered, they are reduced to meat. I left the following morning. By the time I left, the Michigan hunters were on the mountain by themselves. I never saw MGK or his partner again.

The Unwanted Companion

My 1941 Ford pickup died when we returned from the last elk hunt at the ranch. It was no great loss but I needed transportation. I could take my car to the ranch but not on the mountain. In 1958, I purchased a 1957 Chevrolet 1/2-ton pickup. I paid $1400 with 8,000 miles on it. Wow, the places I took that truck! It was a 2 x 4. General Motors did not make 4 x 4's in those early years.

It was good to have a dependable truck for the mountain. The elk season opened in that part of the state on September 10. This had been the opening date for much of the state for decades…my birthday. What could be better than hunting on my birthday?

I was on the mountain the opening day. It was rainy and generally unpleasant. I jumped a bull early in the day but could not get a shot off. Later, several cows spooked and disappeared on a ridge too far to shoot. I returned that night tired, wet and unsuccessful.

I helped Bob with some chores the next morning. The fog and mist were hanging low over the ranch and the nearby river. Bob was often too busy to hunt with me but he would take a day off when he could. By noon, the weather cleared and the sun came out. It was one of those September days in the Wyoming Rockies that are indelibly etched in my memory. I worked until noon. I asked Bob to come and hunt with me but he said that he just could not get away that day and for me go on alone.

Meg fixed us lunch and I packed the few things that I would need to hunt. I started out about 1:30 p.m. The road was slick in places and I was cautious not to take a chance on the narrow canyon rims. The first two miles were the most difficult and they were soon past. I breathed a sigh and continued on. When I was almost to the point where I would begin the hunt, I noticed something in my rear-view mirror. I looked again and then stopped the truck.

It was a dog. A strange looking mongrel, probably part hound and who knows what else. I had seen him once or twice at the ranch but had paid no attention to him. He wasn't the type of dog that would attract any one's attention. He must have been following me clear from the ranch. This had been a long run for him. He was bedraggled, mud covered and severely out of breath. I reached down to pet him but he backed away. What should I do? I didn't want to take him back to the ranch. I still had a mile or two to go. I climbed back in the truck and drove off. He followed me until I stopped again.

He just sat down and watched me as I put on my jacket, loaded my rifle, put my knife and other items in my pockets. I started off toward the nearest ridge. He followed me 30 or 40 feet behind. This began to bother me. I didn't want a dog following me around. Besides it's illegal to use a dog hunting big game. I tried to call him up to me. He would come to within a few feet but would back away at any attempt to touch him.

I decided to ignore the dog as I hunted. He certainly wasn't a warm or welcome companion. After an hour or so, I looked behind me but he was not in sight. I was relieved. Later, I heard a barking in the canyon below me. Was that dog chasing elk?

Later, as I began to change directions high on a ridge, he joined me and walked behind me as if nothing had happened. This began to aggravate me more. He would come and then disappear every hour or so. I sat down to rest on a log. He moved within a few feet and sat and watched me. I started to make a circle back to the truck, down a favorite draw. I had to cross a large windfall area at the lower end. Logs piled on logs and facing in every direction.

Crossing this obstacle course was difficult. Some logs could be stepped over; others had to be climbed over with great effort. I sat on a log to rest. I heard the dog baying now, not barking. It sounded close, just west of me. I was about to leave when I heard some branches breaking from the direction of the baying. A large cow elk was starting across the windfall directly towards me. I waited until she was about 50 yards and broadside. She never saw me. I squeezed off a shot behind the shoulder. When I reached her she was drooping over a log a couple of feet off the ground. She was in a very difficult position. I tried to pull her off and work her between two logs but didn't have the strength. I finally pulled her up on the logs, spread her out and field dressed her on top of them. I was about finished when I looked down and there was the dog watching me. I don't know how long he had been sitting there. He had the strangest look on his face. I reached down and found the liver, cut a large piece of it off, then in smaller pieces and threw it to him. He choked it down as fast as he could and then disappeared. It was getting late and I had a long ways to go. I quickly grabbed my rifle and worked my way back to the truck. The dog was no where in sight.

The next morning I asked Bob to help me get the elk out. It was going to be difficult. It was a hundred yards into the windfall. We hitched up the horse trailer to my pickup, put Whitey, the old white work horse in and headed toward the mountain. On the way out, I spotted that mongrel dog coming across the bridge. I said: "Bob, where did you get that dog?" He responded: "He just showed up one day." I didn't say anything else.

We quartered the elk and took each quarter over and placed it on the pack saddle. We took two quarters out at a time on the horse to the truck. We could have loaded all four, but we needed a rest from dragging them over the windfall.

I left the ranch the next morning. As I drove out, the mongrel dog was sitting by the corner of the bunkhouse. I thought about that dog all winter as I reviewed the hunt in my mind. Had the dog helped me? How and when did he go back to the ranch? Why was he so unfriendly? The next trip up to Dubois, I stopped at the ranch and asked about the dog. Bob said: "I shot him last winter. He was starting to chase cows."

The Wild Bull Ride

My elk hunt of 1959 was different from most of the others as I continued to be successful drawing my permits. There must not have been much competition; I don't think I have won a prize in my life! However, I was always grateful for the privilege and opportunity of hunting in that area. In those days the special permit was a mimeographed post card!

I arrived the morning of the hunt, as usual. Bob Lucas had not hunted much with me for a couple of years. But today, he was in a jovial mood and decided that work could wait and we would hunt together. Bob used an old .30-40 Krag. I think that this was a WWI European Army rifle. But I don't know from which country. It was a good caliber. It had a strange side magazine, with a set of poor iron sights. However, Bob would pull that long barrel up and blast away! He was a pretty good shot.

Bob chose the area that he wanted to hunt. He had been scouting and thought that several bulls had been staying in some thick Jack Pines on the side of a ridge. We took his old Jeep pickup since it was 4 x 4. There was about six inches of snow on the ground from the season's first snow. It almost always snowed during the first ten days of September in that high country. Then there would often be several weeks of wonderful Indian Summer.

We parked the truck on an old logging trail next to the decking area where the logs were piled to be hauled away or sawed by a portable sawmill. We split up and each began to drop down into a deep Jack Pine draw. We had been hiking about 20 minutes when I heard Bob shoot. The sound of that old cannon reverberated off the canyon walls. It had such a distinctive sound.

I continued on for a few minutes down the hill, realizing that Bob could take care of anything that he had shot. Suddenly, I heard this sound coming toward me. I recognized it immediately…a bull running in thick timber. The sounds of a large spooked bull in the timber was like a freight train as the antlers bounced off the trees. Closer and closer it came. I knew it was going to come right by me. I became more nervous. I took the gun off safe and waited. A large bull charged by me. I made the classic mistake of a novice or nervous hunter. I just shot from nervousness and did not aim properly! That bull swerved in front me, not 20 yards away.

I was disgusted and embarrassed. I had hunted many times and seldom made such a mistake. I worked my way towards where I last saw Bob. I found him field dressing a nice, heavy 5 x 5. In that country, the elk were larger than here in Utah, Montana or other areas. There didn't appear to be the small raghorns that are so prevalent now. During those years we killed a lot of 5 x 5's. Most were heavy based and the bodies were large. But, on the other hand we never killed anything larger than 5 x 5. I could never ascertain where the large herd bulls stayed.

I looked at that large, beautiful animal and said: "Do we have to quarter him, and reduce him to just meat, instead of a trophy?" "That's the fastest and easiest way to get him out," Bob mumbled as he tried to cut through the pelvis with an apparently dull old Western Brand hunting knife Finally, out of desperation, he got up, found a rock and started pounding on the back side of the knife. He finished that job and stood up.

"Well, we could go get old Whitey and pull him down the hill." Whitey was the old white work horse, referred to in other stories. Bob said that he would return to the ranch, get the horse, a single tree (this is a wood frame, that pivots, with steel rings to attach a chain) and return in a couple of hours. I told him that I would hunt in the meanwhile, and meet him back at the truck when he returned.

I continued down the ridge where I had missed the bull an hour or so before. It was evident that several elk had spent the last couple of days in the area. Tracks were everywhere, but they had been spooked out of the canyon. I made a circle toward the north, picked up a skid trail and returned to where Bob said he would park the truck. We found a bank where we could back the truck and load the elk at bed level.

The old work horse was not too cooperative as Bob put the harness on him. He wasn't used very much on the ranch, mostly for packing out game. However, he was broke to ride. I can't think of any motivation that could get me to ride him. The three of us followed our tracks back to where the bull was located.

The single tree was about 36 inches long, just the right size. Bob placed the log chain around the base of the antlers, and connected each hook to the rings in the single tree. The chain was a little short and didn't allow much tolerance between the elk and the horse. We started down the skid trail. The grade was modest and it worked for a while. However, the antlers began to turn and twist and dig into the soil, acting like an elk plow. It wasn't going to work and some of the tines might get broken off. Bob yelled: "Whoa," and Whitey was happy to stop.

"We're going to have to do something different," Bob said. "You get on the elk, hold on to the antlers, keep the head up and that will solve our problem." I looked at the elk and the antlers. My better judgment told me not to climb on that elk. However, I realized that I was the one that had made the suggestion to take the elk out whole.

I climbed on the elk. Bob clucked for Whitey to move forward. I pulled hard and lifted. Sure, enough, I could hold the head up and the elk moved smoothly through the snow. This worked for about a hundred yards. Then, we came to a water bar in the trail made for water diversion. The elk slid down, caught up with whitey. I held on tight to the head but it was too late. The antlers pulled from my hand and moved up and gouged

Whitey right up in a very private place. A snort and a blow and he was gone, with me trying to hang on. I yelled: "What shall I do." I could hear Bob faintly say: "Fall off, fall off."

Now, how do you let go of the antlers and fall off? Whitey was moving faster and faster, now the antlers were jabbing him in the lower legs. Each jab caused Whitey to go faster. I became very frightened. The elk was now moving radically sideways, whipping and turning. I closed my eyes and let go. The rear legs of the elk brushed me as I slipped over them.

The speed of my departure threw me into a tree on the edge of the trail. I hit right on the side of my rib cage, My hat was gone and I was covered with snow and pine needles. Otherwise, no worse for wear! Bob picked up my hat as he came running down the trail. "Are you okay, are you okay?" I stood up, breathless, rubbing my side. "I'm okay, but what about Whitey and the elk?" "Don't worry, the horse'll stop at the bottom of the hill," Bob said.

Our pace was slow as we walked down the hill. I began to limp from a charley horse. I stopped, rubbed intently and then we proceeded to where the Pickup was parked. There stood Whitey, head down, still panting, his breath showing in the cold mountain air. I ran to look at the antlers of the elk. Not a single tine was broken. However, they looked a lot better; they had been polished all the way down the hill.

We loosened the elk and together, with great effort, pushed it into the pickup, with the head forward. The elk filled that Jeep Pickup. The antlers touched each side of the bed. What a photo that would have made but I had forgotten my camera. Speaking of photos, some were available of these experiences; some have been lost and some were never taken!

We hitched the horse trailer back to the pickup, put Whitey in and started down the hill. Bob said: "If you had not missed that bull we could have pulled two of them down that hill." I rubbed my side. I didn't think it was very humorous.

Above, old Whitey, the horse that gave the author the wild bull ride. Below, Bob Lucas skins out the bull elk, Wyoming, 1959.

We returned to the ranch and took care of Whitey. Bob took the old John Deer tractor and lifted out the elk. A magnificent bull. Why did I have to *miss my bull?* The answer was, of course, what drives men to hunt...the thrill of the stalk; the risk of missing; the joy of sharing; the agony of ridicule from your friends. We spent the afternoon skinning and preparing the elk.

Bob gave me the skin. This was the first elk hide, whole, that I had ever obtained. I had it tanned and later would trade that hide to a friend to customize my .30-06.

Meg fixed us dinner as she cared for her, by now, three small children. One, named Clark, crawled around the floor as we ate. I picked him up, loved him and thought, "If I ever have any boys, I think I'll name one Clark." This did happen, I named my second son Clark Proud Mahaffey.

By now, every bone in my body ached. I began to wonder if I had cracked some ribs. My lower back ached, even my head ached! At 8:30 p.m., I dismissed myself and limped to the bunk house and climbed into my sagging bed.

The new day dawned beautiful, bright and sunny. The bull was hanging in an old shed. Bob was pleased for the meat. Sometimes I gave him my elk. He and his hired hands used a lot of meat. I had two more days before having to return to Casper.

I had slept well, but now was very sore. I thought a good walk might loosen up those tight muscles. But I couldn't figure out how a walk could help my sore rib cage. But undaunted, I told Bob that I was going to drive up the mountain again and find my elk. He said: "Go ahead, but I have other things to do."

About 9:00 a.m., I took my Chevy pickup and drove across the bridge and up the mountain. Crossing that old, sagging wood bridge, acted as a threshold, and when crossed, excitement came, no matter how many times the ritual occurred.

I didn't want to hunt where we had hunted before. I didn't want to hunt west where I killed my first elk years before. I decided that I would hunt the "bull pasture." This was an enduring title to a long draw that I had walked many, many times. Seldom did I not at least see a bull, and often I, or other hunters bagged one bull at a time from that draw.

I started up one side of the draw, intending to come down the other side. One hunter could not cover the whole draw and elk would often drift from one side to the other, if disturbed. I saw elk sign all way up the draw, but nothing looked very fresh. It is often difficult to tell the age of elk sign in the snow. However, urine and feces can be good indicators of the age of the sign. On damp mornings, with no wind, elk can easily be smelled. They have a dank, acrid smell common to cattle feed yards.

I traversed the whole draw, topped the ridge, looked south into the great draws and canyons that seemed to go on forever. I turned and started down the east side. That side of the draw had been logged over and much of the debris was still there. It takes centuries for the slash of logging to deteriorate at high elevations. Those areas were attractive to elk, especially as the new growth moved in. The feed and cover were prime areas for elk. I saw very little sign and began to think that I would not see anything this time in the bull pasture.

I neared the bottom of the draw where all of the skid trails converged, where the logs were decked and cut. I looked all around as I began to walk to a major road and then back to the truck. On the west side was a huge sawdust pile. I didn't pay much attention, but then I saw a movement and, right on top of that pile, was a large cow and her calf. I missed seeing her at first, her yellow rump and dark brown sides were about the same color as the aged, stained sawdust.

She made a good target at 90 yards, I pulled up, off hand, and shot her in the neck. The calf began to move away. I remembered one of Bob's hired hands mentioned that he had a permit and could use some meat. I squeezed off another shot. There would be plenty of meat for the ranch.

I field dressed each animal and started off toward the pickup. I drove right to the sawdust pile, quartered each animal and returned to the ranch. Bob and everyone was pleased for my success. Bob said: "Why didn't you come and get Whitey and pull them out? Then, he continued by saying I can't figure out why you can hit cows but not bulls."

The Great Bear Robbery

Bears had always fascinated me, especially in my early years of hunting. I often saw sign, followed their tracks but never could see one. My interest in bears was tremendously increased from some of my trips to Alaska. I have seen the inland Grizzly at Mount Dinali and many great Alaska Brown Bears along the rivers and streams. My primary hunting fantasy…unfulfilled…is shooting a bear.

On several of my elk hunts with Bob Lucas, we discussed the possibility of bear hunting. Bob had seen several and had shot at a couple but the old .30-40 Krag didn't deliver. Bears were open game during the fall season and could also be hunted in the spring. Most bears were killed while stalking other animals. However, those killed in the spring were attracted by using bait. Bait can be any dead animal or other carrion that develops an odor that will attract the bear. The best bait is a dead horse or cow.

When I left the ranch after hunting elk in 1959, Bob said that we would try to hunt bear in the spring. He would save the first dead steer or horse and use it for bait. I called him in April to remind him of the agreement. He said he had a couple of cows that had died during the winter and they could be used. He promised to take the tractor, load one in his pickup and place it in a good place.

One day in the middle of May he called me and told me the bait had been put out and to come up and we would hide in a blind and see what happened. I was excited to go to the ranch for any reason and a chance to hunt bear was a bonus. The bait was watched in the evening when the bears came in to feed. Once they start feeding, they will often come in for several nights unless disturbed. Bob told me that there had been some tracks around the bait.

I drove up one Saturday afternoon. We visited and then made our trek up the mountain. He had put the bait out south of Old Baldy, on the side of a ridge. It looked like a pretty good place to hunt. The bait should be placed on the edge of the timber or in a clearing so it is in clear sight from the blind. The blind can be anything to hide the hunters. Even an animal as large as a cow or horse has to be staked tightly to the ground or the bear will drag it away. Bob had the cow tied down with a large chain attached to two pipe stakes.

We arrived an hour before dark. There had been tracks around the bait but it had not been disturbed much. The weather had been cold and there was a lot of snow left on the north slopes. A bear is often attracted by the maggots and will feed on them first. However, this bait didn't have many maggots. The weather was too cold for flies to reproduce themselves.

Our blind was a pile of logs, with some pine boughs to cover the open areas. I hunkered down as the temperature began to drop. The sun was down and we could feel the cold air beginning to fall into the valley. I had on a heavy coat but sitting on the side of a hill in May in the high country is not exactly comfortable. Bob and I didn't say much. We had no idea which way a bear would come. Logic might indicate a bear would come in from the lee side, after smelling the bait. But a wandering bear could come in from any direction.

The light began to dim and nothing happened. Then I punched Bob and pointed to a movement coming down the ridge, slightly below the tree line. It looked black and was moving at a moderate pace. It was going directly toward the bait. I knew that this might be my chance. It disappeared behind some trees, reappeared and then was gone again. Then, it showed up, right in front of us by the bait. I threw up my gun and scoped it...a cow moose!

Sweet disappointment. The light was about gone by now. Bob and I got up and began our walk back to the truck, and then on down to the ranch. We drove slowly. The old Jeep pickup had one light out and the other was pretty dim. We didn't want to go off in a canyon while missing one of the sharp turns.

We tried again the next night with the same results. I had to leave on Monday morning in time to return to Casper for the night shift at the newspaper. I told Bob that I wanted a bear but that I couldn't keep running up here with such poor results. He promised me that he would watch the bait and wait until he knew that a bear was coming in regularly. I agreed and returned home.

Bob called me one night in late May. He had watched the bait for five days and it appeared that the bear was coming in each night. About half of the cow had been eaten. That was great news. I told Bob that I would be there day after tomorrow in time to hunt in the evening.

This was it. We had it figured out this time. The bear would be there.

I was excited. The next day I prepared everything for the trip. That afternoon I received a call from Bob, shortly before leaving for work. "I have bad news," he said. "Don't bother to come up tomorrow." I said: "Why, what happened?" "The bear's already been shot, but I didn't do it. Two kids from that ranch over on Warm Springs found out about the bait and shot it last night." Then adding to my disappointment, Bob continued: "It was a big black boar. It weighed about 500 pounds." It was too late in the year to put out another bait. I talked about hunting bear the next spring but Bob didn't seem interested.

The Addict

By 1961, things were changing at the ranch and in my life. In 1962, Bob and his family moved to Hudson, Wyoming and he took employment at a recently opened taconite mine. Although he loved the ranch, he could not make a living there, especially with three children and their economic demands.

In 1957, I completed my apprenticeship and became a journeyman printer. I continued to work at the *Casper Morning Star*. At this time I realized that my future was not in printing. This feeling was strengthened by changing technology. In 1959 I became a student at Casper College. I finished the two-year program in 1961. We sold every-thing, including my cherished Chevy pickup, and began school at Colorado State University. I did not hunt the fall of 1961. I had just finished a summer term high in the mountains of Colorado and had not applied for a special permit.

The summer of 1962, I worked for the Rocky Mountain Forest and Range Experiment Station, out of Fort Collins, Colorado. I traveled to several states gathering research information on visitors to National Forest Service recreational areas. This was of great value to me as I learned to observe human behavior from various social and psychological viewpoints. It even helped me analyze my own behavior!

I wanted to return to the ranch and hunt elk that fall. However, I didn't have any transportation. By then I had a 1960 Rambler Station Wagon, and

131

my wife, Barbara needed it to use for work. However, I had faith and applied for the permit. I was still a legal resident of Wyoming, even though I was living out of state.

I spent a week at a time in various National Forests conducting the research. One week, I was working in South Dakota, near Custer State Park and near Rushmore National park. I was visiting with a couple at a campground. They were middle aged but the husband had MS and wore a brace on his back for stability. They were from Cheyenne, Wyoming. He had a medical disability from some government agency.

The subject of hunting came up and then elk hunting in particular. He had hunted deer but had never hunted elk before. He told me that, at home, he had a new International Scout. The Scout was about the first version of what we now call "sport utility vehicle," and was 4 x 4. I quickly solved three problems in my mind: the Scout, my need for transportation, and his desire to hunt elk. I told him there was still time to apply for a special permit. If he received it, he could provide the transportation. I would be his guide and he could have, perhaps, his last chance for an elk hunt before he became a complete invalid.

He wrote me a few weeks later that he had, indeed, been successful in the draw for the permit. I was excited until I began to think about how I was going to help a semi-invalid hunt elk high in the Rockies of Wyoming. However, we made our plans. I was to travel to Cheyenne and we would use the Scout from that point. I would have to do all of the driving but I didn't mind. That Scout was nice! But by today's standards, it was primitive.

Since Bob Lucas had left the ranch, I didn't know where to stay. I really didn't want to camp out with Tom, and his MS problems, although he was willing. I then remembered, several miles west of our familiar hunting area, was an old line shack, used for decades by local cowboys, as they wrangled the cows on their Forest Service Allotments. We would gamble that it would be vacant and use it. I thought that it had a stove and the other essentials. However, it had been several years since I had seen it.

I was concerned whether I could get across the bridge at the ranch, since Bob was no longer there. How I missed his friendship and the security of knowing that I would always have access. We arrived at mid-day, the day before the opening of the season. I quietly drove by the ranch. There didn't appear to be anyone around. I pulled upon the old wood bridge. The gate was not closed and so I drove across the mental threshold of another hunting experience!

The Scout was not large. I determined that if we were successful, there was enough room for our elk, if quartered. I had never tried the 4 x 4 feature. I put it in and took it out a couple of times to get used to it. We came to the crossroads of Bald Mountain, or Old Baldy as most of us referred to it. I had tried to take my Chevy up a couple of times, but without 4 x 4, I didn't get to the top. The trail was narrow, winding and steep.

I asked Tom if he wanted to get a great view of the valley, not telling him that I was about to give the Scout a "baptism" of performance. He said: "No problem," which was not necessarily prophetic. We drove until I had to put it into the special 4 x 4 gears. Wow, what power. We began to make the upper switchbacks, back and forth in hairpin turns. This thing could go anywhere! We were almost to the top when I thought that I would stop at an angle where Tom could see the great view. From there you could look directly down on the small town of Dubois, perhaps 10 or 12 miles below.

I slowly stopped. Tom was on the outside, over the edge of the trail. I stopped and then felt a strange sensation. The Scout was rocking, or should I say teetering. A sick feeling came to me. I had just made a discovery that was kept a secret for years: this model of Scout was notoriously top heavy! I sat very still as Tom looked over the country. I was afraid he would look at me and see how frightened I was.

We were almost on top of Old Baldy, where I could turn around and start down. However, the grade was very steep and were going sideways. At this elevation, there were no trees, some brush, but mostly grass and rock debris. What should I do? Tom appeared unperturbed and apparently didn't feel the rocking. If I continued ahead and hit a rock or if the trail increased in grade, we might roll all the way down the mountain side. I had to get the Scout pointing directly down. But how?

I said: "Tom, this is a good view, I don't think I'll go on to the top. I think that I'll just work my way down from here." I started ahead slowly. Should I go faster? As I moved forward, I slowly turned left and tried to point the Scout *down*. It rocked slightly and then made the turn. Now what? Straight down and no trail. I shifted to the lowest gear and it whined, even with my foot firmly on the brakes. The wheels locked and we began a slow skid. I took the brakes off slightly and we would roll ahead. Loose rock and shale started rolling down the hill. We continued this process for about 200 yards until we crossed the next switchback. From there, we had no problem getting back to the crossroads.

I stopped the Scout and said: "What did you think about that view?" Tom sighed and said: "That was one of the most beautiful views I have seen." I removed the 4 x 4 and started toward the cabin. I felt some drops of perspiration drip down inside my flannel shirt.

I knew where not to go with the Scout. I began to worry and have reservations about how it would perform in other situations. However, I was not going to give it any more performance tests unless I had to. We pulled up to the cabin. It looked empty. I was greatly relieved. Now we have already discussed the importance of hunting cabins. This was one of those cabins that had the "welcome" look. The inside and outside were covered with an old Celotex type material. It was fine for inside but would not last too long in the weather. The outside was stained and marked by the depth of the snow banks from previous winters.

I pushed open the door. Just like home! There was the all-important cooking and heating stove, two bunks with no mattresses a table and a bench. What else could we need? There were a few sticks of wood in the wood box and a few provisions on a shelf on the wall. It was the general rule to leave the wood box full and as many provisions as possible for emergency use. But apparently, the last users weren't concerned.

I took an old broom and swept out the pine needles and other debris on the floor. We definitely would not have to worry about muddy shoes in this cabin. I cut wood, unpacked and put all of our gear in order. Tom could do a lot of work, considering his disability. I was impressed. He was kind, cooperative and congenial that afternoon and evening. After supper, before dark, I took a walk down the trail to where it joined a creek running through the canyon. This cabin was at the end of the road to the west. From there on, one had to take a horse or walk.

There were a lot of cows along the creek. The summer allotment usually lasted until October 1st, unless bad weather forced the cows down before that time. Today was September 9; tomorrow would be my birthday. We watched the remains of a glorious sunset through some distant low clouds. The weather looked promising for the next day. No snow had fallen yet. There was usually a snow storm during the first two weeks of September in this high country. The thought made me a little nervous...even though we had a Scout.

I had been wondering for weeks how I would help Tom hunt. I had not been around him enough to evaluate his physical condition. His wife didn't say anything to me when we left, just smiled and waved. But now I had to make some decisions. He told me that he didn't want me to "nurse him." I asked him what that meant. He said he could hunt by himself and could walk for a mile or so. I then tried to figure out where I could take him with those limitations. A mile in the high country is more than most hunters realize and most distances are over stated.

Then a thought came to me. The Bull Pasture. The perfect place. It was easy walking and I could drive him to the beginning of the canyon, and could pick him up for that matter, if we could coordinate our activities. I was greatly relieved. I lit our Coleman Lantern: we heated some water and had hot chocolate before climbing into our mattressless bunks. Fortunately, I had brought two pieces of foam which reduced the discomfort from the exposed springs.

We were up early, had a great breakfast and prepared to leave. I could hear some cattle lowing in the distance. In past years in this area, I had seen moose grazing with the cows. I mentioned to Tom to watch for moose and don't confuse them with either cows or elk.

I drove him a quarter mile to the beginning of the Bull Pasture. I repeated several times where to go and where to turn around. I told him not to get exhausted and to be cautious of his footing, especially in going across the creek and in the bogs. I felt a tinge of responsibility, as he struggled to get out. I handed him his gun, asked him about a knife, water, etc. He appeared to be well prepared. He was shooting a Winchester .270, an adequate caliber for elk. I forgot to ask him if he had ever field dressed an animal.

I was unsure of where to hunt. I wanted to go about two miles east to some of my more favored areas but thought better of it since I would be so far from Tom. Instead, on an impulse, I stopped at the next draw east of where Tom would be hunting.

It was a similar draw to the Bull Pasture, but not as long and the cover was not as good. I had seen elk there before but not often. I stopped, picked up my gun, and other gear and started down an intermittent creek. It was dry that year. The creek usually had running water, especially after a snow. I looked for sign but saw none. The dry pine needles made tracking very difficult. Instead of tracking, I would move quietly through the best areas. I worked my way back and forth across the creek, through bogs and down timber. After an hour I heard bang, bang, bang. I knew that Tom had, at least, seen something. I was pleased. Hopefully, he would not get hurt. My first instincts were to work my way over the ridge back to Tom, but then "he didn't want nursed."

I continued on, rapidly gaining elevation. I stopped to rest in a pleasant old growth fir and spruce park. I had not seen a track. As I arose, I noticed a movement below me. I moved quickly down to get a better view. I looked. Two spikes. What are two spikes doing together? I continued to move sideways to get a better view. The nearest one was moving to my right, full broadside at 80 yards. I aimed for his neck, squeezed off the shot. I was still using the 150-grain bullet in my .30-06. The young bull dropped like a rock. The other one spooked and ran to the right. I could hear him as he crossed some downed timber.

I worked my way over to where I thought the spike went down. I couldn't find him. I walked back and forth for a hundred yards in every direction. I looked for blood. I could faintly make out tracks in the dry pine needles but nothing else. A lost elk. It is difficult to explain the frustration of a hunter losing an animal that has been hit. I would much rather have a clean miss rather than lose an animal if it has been wounded. However, this is part of the hunting experience.

I quickly quit hunting and returned to the truck. I drove back to the cabin. Tom had not returned. It was 11:00. He should have been here by now. I fixed some lunch and began to become increasingly worried. I decided that if he had not returned by 2:00, I would go looking for him. At 1:30, heard someone yell "Come, help me, come help me." I quickly ran out and down the road to where I thought the sound was coming. In front of me was a large range bull and several cows blocking the road. Behind them was Tom, with the whole head of a small 5 x 5 bull on his shoulders. I scattered the cows off the road and ran to him and lifted the heavy head from his shoulders.

He was exhausted. I could understand. He had carried that head through the pasture and up the road to the cabin. I threw the head down on he porch of the cabin, took Tom in and sat him down. He was trembling and his face was snow white. He said: "I have to take my medicine now." He disappeared toward his bunk. I fixed him some lunch. He immediately became calm, and began to babble out his experiences of the morning. He had jumped the single bull at 60 yards, missed him the first two times but scored a hit behind the shoulder on the third shot. The rest of the morning had been spent field dressing and cutting off the head with his knife. By late afternoon Tom was in his bunk sleeping.

I looked at his emaciated body, his chest heaving with heavy breathing. I looked at the full length, upper torso body brace that he wore. He must have weighed barely more than 100 pounds. How did he carry that bull head that distance? I thought about going out hunting for the evening but decided against it. I would fix a nice dinner for the both of us. I wished that Tom had brought back the liver but that would have been more weight and difficult to carry. I usually carry the liver on a stick with a fork at the end to keep it from slipping off.

I went to our cooler, got out two beef steaks, a couple of potatoes, some onions and prepared to fix dinner. I started the fire and the cabin took on a friendly, warm atmosphere, in spite of the austere interior. By the time I had finished cooking everything, Tom had awakened and slowly got off his bunk. He looked so weak and tired. He said: "I must take my medicine," and turned his back to me.

Together, we ate both steaks, and all of the potatoes, onions, green beans and canned peaches. I have just described the typical dinner for hunters across the nation! However, when I was a kid hunting with Dave, eating the liver after the first kill and for every meal until leaving was a standard procedure. *Every one* ate liver, whether they liked it or not. Actually, I have always liked liver, but it must be sauteed with onions.

We visited a little while after dinner and then it grew dark. I boiled some water. Water has to be boiling on a wood cook stove even if you don't have any use for it. I made us each a cup of hot chocolate. Tom still looked pale, but he began to talk with enthusiasm about many things, some of which didn't make too much sense to me. His mood swings became evident *after* he took his medicine.

But we had a few laughs before I turned out the light and crawled into my sleeping bag. A crippled up victim of MS had killed a 5 x 5 bull. I, a healthy, strong, experienced hunter could not kill a bull, broadside, at 80 yards. I decided that in the morning, I would go back through the draw that I hunted today, cross over the ridge and come back by way of the Bull Pasture.

I awakened before Tom, got up and started the fire. It was cold in the cabin. I looked out and saw a heavy frost on the Scout and over the whole valley. Tom could hardly say a word when he got up. He looked so tired and weak. He staggered around for a few minutes, mumbled that he would take his medicine and then sat down on the bench in front of the stove. I told him that I was going to hunt for a few more hours. I asked him if he thought we could work the Scout up the draw and pick up the elk. He said he didn't know.

I told Tom to relax and that I would be back by noon. I decided that I would walk to the draw instead of taking the Scout. I grabbed my rifle, jacket, some jerky, a small can of beans and was on my way. A beautiful day. I passed some of the cows that remained in the valley from the day before. I started up the draw on the opposite side from the route taken the day before. I still saw no sign. I had hunted about 30 minutes and was walking along the creek for sign when I heard a branch snap. I looked up and crossing the creek above me was a spike bull.

I jumped up on the bank to get a shot at him. He didn't seem spooked. I worked my way over to a tree, leaned against it and scoped him. He looked just likes the ones from the day before. An 18-inch spike. I slowly and deliberately placed the cross hair on his neck, then remembering the day before, I moved it behind the shoulder. He was beginning to get nervous and was walking at an angle away. I squeezed off the shot. He jumped, appeared hit, reared and ran down the creek. I watched as he plunged a few more yards and collapsed. By the time I reached him, he was dead. I field dressed him but did not quarter him.

I looked around me. How can I get the Scout in here? It will be very difficult, but not impossible. I would have to drive over one questionable bog across the creek, perhaps cut a tree or two and then the way would be easy.

I walked out the way that I would have to drive in, came up on the road and returned to the cabin. When I entered the cabin, Tom was sitting at the table, with a strange look on his face. He began to babble: "We are going to die here. We can't get out. Help me, help me. There's no way. It's hopeless," and other meaningless phrases.

He looked so pathetic. I didn't know what medicine he was taking, but he needed some now! "Have you taken your medicine," I asked. "Medicine," he questioned. "Yes, whatever it is that you take," I replied.

"Oh, yes, medicine, yes medicine." He said as he got up and staggered over to his bunk where his personal gear was in a small bag. I watched closely this time as he prepared the syringe and injected himself. In a few minutes, he began to look better and talked to me. I told him of my success, he seemed pleased but said that he wanted to go home soon.

I asked him if he could go with me to help me work the Scout to my elk. He said yes. He slowly climbed into the Scout and sat beside me. He didn't say much as I worked my way to the creek, found a place to cross and moved on. I then cut one tree off at the ground with a hand saw, and within a few minutes pulled up beside the spike. In a few more minutes, I had it quartered and in the Scout.

After returning to the cabin, I asked him if he could find his bull. He said that he thought so, but would have to walk ahead first. I worried about this but he walked and guided me to the bull. The body was larger than the antlers would indicate. It was located on the side of a small rise. I would have to carry the quarters for a few yards. I told Tom to sit down and I would bring the Scout. I carefully returned the way that I would drive up the draw. I scraped one fender a little but in a few minutes had returned.

Tom sat, motionless, as he watched me work on his elk. The body was very stiff by now and I had a hard time. I was using an ax to split the backbone and it was difficult. I hesitated to ask his help, but I finally completed the task. He had done a good job of field dressing the animal but had not split the pelvis or the rib cage.

We now had two elk in the Scout and the back was full. We would have to put a lot of the camping gear in the back seat but that would be no problem. I told Tom when we returned that it was too late to start today and that we would start out for home early in the morning. He reluctantly agreed, went into the cabin and collapsed on his bunk. I spent the afternoon and evening packing the Scout. The weather was cold enough that I didn't think I would have to hang the elk that night, although my elk was not well cooled. Proper cooling is critical to ensure protection of the meat .

We had canned chili for supper. I ate mine but Tom picked at his. I counted the hours since his last medicine. I asked him: "Do you think it's time to take your medicine." "Yes, it's time," he responded, and moved across the cabin. I was hopeful that he had enough to get us back to Cheyenne tomorrow.

We awakened early, ate, packed our gear and were ready to start down to the ranch, Dubois and then Cheyenne. I cleaned the cabin and filled the wood box. I looked in our grocery box, selected some cans of soup, beans and peaches and placed them on the shelf. I used the old broom to sweep the floor. Tom was in the Scout as I slowly closed the door and walked across the porch. I would never enter that cabin again.

The author, sitting on the porch of the old Celotex covered cabin. Note the 5 x 5 antlers bagged by the 'Addict,' Wyoming, 1961.

Tom was in a better mood as we approached the ranch. I slowly pulled across the bridge. There was a pickup at the barn, I looked over and waved and drove on to the highway.

Tom slept some on the way back to Cheyenne. I called Barbara and told her when I would be arriving at Cheyenne. It was an hour's drive from Fort Collins. I made sure that he took his medicine every four or five hours. He became more enthused as we neared Cheyenne. We pulled up in his driveway. His wife came running out and asked us how we did. Tom proudly showed his elk antlers.

We unpacked the Scout. Just as we were finishing, Barbara pulled into the driveway. I put my elk and the camping gear in the Rambler. I was ready to leave. Tom walked down the driveway. I met him; I thanked him for going with me. He said he enjoyed the trip. He put a limp hand in mine; I squeezed it lightly, turned and walked away. I never saw or heard from Tom again.

The Missing Glove

During the summer of 1963, I worked for the Roosevelt National Forest out of Fort Collins, Colorado, where I was going to school at Colorado State University. I had a job where I traveled the National Forest, doing interpretive work with the public. I had planned to graduate during December of that year. I knew that I would be moving to some other state, probably not Wyoming.

These thoughts prompted a "one more hunt" feeling about the ranch and the Shoshone National Forest. I had a friend, with whom I worked at the *Casper Morning Star*. His name was Charles Ridgeway. I had hunted with him several years before. He had a 4 x 4 pickup and he had expressed some interest in hunting elk with me the last time I visited with him. Another long time friend, Terry Beaver from Tekamah, Nebraska had also expressed some interest. I used to work with Terry and had hunted with him many times. In fact, he shot me once, but that is another story!

We all drew our permits. Our plans were made. I would drive up from Fort Collins; Terry would drive over from Tekamah; we would meet at Casper and join up with Charles. I recall I almost missed getting my permit. Although I was legally a resident of Wyoming, I feared that an out-of-state address would confuse the bureaucrats. But about the time the permits were to be mailed out, I could not remember whose address I used on the forms. I contacted the Wyoming G&F and asked them about the address. Their response was typical: "If you don't know where you live, we can't help you." I finally realized that I had used the address of a friend and I retrieved the permit.

We consolidated all of our gear into two vehicles at Casper. We bought groceries and assembled everything that I thought that we would need. I was concerned where we would stay. I told the others that the old cabin would "probably" be available to us.

I was interested in the pickup that we would be using. It was the first model International 1/2-ton 4 x 4 on the market. It looked worn out but still usable, at least for one more trip. I asked Charles: "How's it run?" He responded: "Great, but there's a little problem with the steering. It won't turn very sharp to the right." "Won't turn to the right, I questioned?" "Sharp to the right," he said. I became more cautious: "What's sharp to the right mean?" Charles was getting a little testy from my questions. "Don't worry about it, let's go," Charles said as he climbed up and worked at the door handle until it finally opened. As we drove out of Casper, I tried to count the number of curves to the right that we would be making on that narrow road up the mountain.

We arrived at Dubois in the early afternoon. I slowed down as I approached the ranch. It looked abandoned, but I didn't want to stop to find out. Fortunately, this was a sharp turn to the left and the pickup worked fine. We pulled across the wood bridge for what would be my last time. The same thrill came to me as I looked across the Wind River.

We wound our way up the mountain as I had done so many times before and worked our way southwest to where the old cabin was located. On the sharp turns to the right, Charles would have to back up and turn and then back up and turn until he could finally make a turn of the necessary circumference. At first, it was aggravating, but we soon got used to it. Charles became so confident that he could look at the curve and determine, ahead of time, how many maneuvers that it would take to get around the right hand curves.

The road was rough but dry. No snow had yet fallen that fall. We came around the curve approaching the cabin. I looked ahead and two pickups were parked in front of it. We slowly passed the cabin so that we could turn around. If there were people inside, they didn't come out. Tears came to my eyes. I almost felt violated as we drove away. I have never been back. I have often wondered if that old Celotex covered cabin still exists.

Well, we had a problem: where to camp. We didn't even bring a wall tent. We did have a couple of tarps and a small umbrella tent in which to sleep. But where would we cook, rest and eat? Then a thought came to me. I remembered an old camp site that I had passed many times. It had an old pole tent frame and a corral. There was a spring that ran through the corral. In fact, we had kept the old horse Whitey in the corral.

We arrived and the old camp was just as I remembered it. We put up the umbrella tent next to the frame. We combined the tarps and they were big enough to cover half of the frame. We had some shelter. We could build a fire for heat. We had a Coleman stove for cooking. This wasn't my cabin, but we could survive. Terry and Charles were good sports and we all pitched in and arranged our gear.

We shared the cooking chores that night. We built a rip-snorting fire. There was plenty of firewood around the old campsite. As soon as darkness came, so did the cold air as it engulfed the valley floor. We sat around the fire for a few minutes and then headed for the sleeping bags. I continued to lament about the lost cabin. Terry said: "Forget the cabin, we'll have fun right here." As we snuggled into our bags, we discussed how we would hunt the next day. Terry did not feel comfortable taking off by himself in strange country…especially being a flatlander. So he and I would hunt together. Charles said I could point out a ridge for him to walk in the morning. I thought about the Bull Pasture, but it was too close to the other hunters in the cabin.

It was cold in the morning. I got up, built a fire and pumped up the Coleman stove. Now, we use propane; what an improvement it is over the old white gas pressure system. I was going to wash my face, but there was a skim of ice on the bucket. I had a better idea, as I put some water on the stove to boil. By the time breakfast was over, I was shivering from the cold.

The three of us started out together. I made sure each person had some lunch. I didn't worry about water. In those days we were not concerned about Girardia and all of the other modern health scares. We walked down the main road to where a skid trail intersected. I pointed out the ridge that Charles should follow. He was enthused and walked off at a brisk pace. Charles was shooting some kind of generic brand .30-06. It would be adequate, if he could hit anything.

Both Terry and I were shooting .30-06's, but his was a Remington and mine was a Winchester. Terry and I started in the opposite direction from Charles. I knew exactly where I wanted to go to complete a long, arduous circle back to the camp. I didn't give much consideration to Terry's physical condition or to the type of boots he was wearing.

Terry and I walked almost continuously all day. Up ridges and down valleys and then parallel to timberline. We stopped for lunch, spread out and rested. We didn't walk together, but usually about 50-100 yards apart when appropriate. We both enjoyed the hunt. However, I am sure we made too much noise for serious stalking. That is a problem with hunting closely with someone. The concern and constant need for communication adds to the burden of an effective, silent stalk. We had not seen an animal of any kind.

We topped the last long ridge and draw. I thought that our camp was at the base of this draw. On clear days, keeping oriented was easy, but cloudy days can cause some serious problems. This was a bright, clear day and I was thankful. As we started down the hill, I noticed that Terry seemed to be limping. However, he had not said anything during the day about any discomfort.

Terry was walking about 50 yards to my right. I was getting extremely tired and was shuffling along at a easy pace. I saw a movement below me, next to the heavy timber. A huge bull elk was moving out of the draw and heading toward the timber. As he entered, I noted how he threw his antlers back over his shoulders, with his nose held high, as he entered the timber. I could hear the rattle of the antlers against the trees as he disappeared.

I quickly motioned to Terry, violently pointing down the draw. Then I held arms up wide to indicate the size of the elk. He quickly came alive and began to run toward me. We stopped and I explained what I had seen. I told him that I would drop down through the timber and that he should remain right on the edge, in case the elk should come out again.

I had an extremely difficult time getting through all of the windfall on the side of the ridge. But I finally emerged at the bottom. Terry was standing in the middle of a skid trail when I emerged. Neither of us had seen or heard a thing.

We were disappointed but, at least, we had seen an elk. We continued on down the trail. In a few minutes I recognized where I was. This was the right ridge and we were soon at our camp site. Charles was sitting under the tarp around the old stumps that we were using for a table, sharing the constant grin that he carried with him.

Terry sat down and immediately took off his boots. I collapsed on the ground. What a hike! Terry and I began to argue about how far we had walked and then the argument changed to who would be responsible for cooking supper. We finally compromised and agreed that we all would make some kind of labor contribution.

I was peeling potatoes, Charles was trying to light a heating fire. Suddenly Charles turned around, looked at us and said: "Aren't you going to ask me how I did today?" I said, "Okay, how did you do today?" To my astonishment, he said: "I killed a 4 x 4 clear on top of the ridge that I was walking."

Terry and I gave a forced laugh at this, thinking he was joking. But, we soon realized he was serious and asked him to tell us the story. Charles said that he had worked his way up and across the ridge but didn't see any sign or hear anything. At about 11:00, he topped out and rested for a few minutes and walked along the top and dropped down off a ledge, intending to circle back.

Charles was a rock hound and loved to polish rocks. He came across a talus slope. He laid down his gun and began a serious exploration of all of the rock debris. He looked here and there at different specimens. He pick up a large rock, looked at it and heaved it out of the way. For some reason he glanced to see where the rock landed. About 20 yards from where the rock landed, a 4 x 4 bull was intently watching his movements. Charles walked over, picked up his gun and shot it behind the shoulder. It ran a few yards and dropped. What a story. I said: "However, you can't keep this bull. It is illegal to hunt elk while hunting rocks at the same time." In reality, Terry and I were pleased for his success. I felt a tinge of envy.

We finished dinner, cleaned up the pans and dishes, boiled some water and talked for a few minutes. By now, I was totally exhausted. I glanced at Terry. He looked like warmed over death and so I suggested that we go to bed and we would make plans for tomorrow over breakfast.

I was the first up, as usual, but much later than the morning before. I started the morning chores. It didn't seem as cold today. However, there was a heavy frost on the meadows. A few rays from the morning sun sparkled as they reflected off the frosty logs and grass. Charles finally got up. Terry and I were finishing breakfast. As Charles staggered out of the tent, with two days of heavy black beard showing, he might have been confused with an early mountain man in this very valley! But he would have been a small mountain man. He was only about 5'4" tall.

I suggested that Charles return and quarter the elk and try to find some route to get as close as possible. We didn't have a horse and would have to carry each quarter out. I asked him if he thought he could find it again. Charles indicated that it would not be any problem.

I decided that Terry and I would take a similar but shorter route and traverse some smaller ridges lower in the valley. I was putting on my jacket and packing my gear when Terry said: "My feet are killing me. My boots were not broken in. I want to stay in camp today and clean it up. You go on ahead without me." I had mixed emotions. I was his host. We lost our cabin, hadn't gotten a shot and now he was disabled.

On the positive side, I would not be handicapped by having him along, as much as I wanted to help him. He didn't appear to be too upset.

Walking with blisters or boots that don't fit can be very painful. I picked up my rifle, gloves, lunch and said goodbye to both and started down a long skid trail parallel to the road that we came in.

I walked a few hundred yards, remembered that I should put a shell in my chamber. I pumped in a shell, put one glove on and looked for the other glove. I couldn't find it. I went through all pockets twice. I must have dropped it on the trail. I knew that I had both gloves when I started out at camp.

My hand was cold and so I decided that it wouldn't be that much trouble to retrace my footsteps and find the glove. It was a new, yellow, leather glove and would be easy to find on the trail. I walked briskly back, watching closely. There it was, crumpled on the trail. I reached down, picked it up and started to put it on. In so doing, I glanced over toward the timber along side of the trail, about 60 yards. Looking right at me, was a large bull elk!

I didn't finish putting on the glove. I snapped my safety off and pulled the gun up to my shoulder. The elk had turned slightly as if going to turn around. My shot slammed him right behind his right front shoulder. I heard the "splat" that is characteristic on some shots. The bull whirled and was gone. I quickly pumped in another shell, reached down, picked my the empty brass, and my glove that had dropped again during the excitement.

I started toward the place he disappeared in the timber. Suddenly, I stopped. I remembered reading an article a few days before in *Outdoor Life* by Jack O'Connor or some famous hunter-writer. According to the author, if you know that you have hit an animal and it runs, sit down for 15 minutes, have a cigarette and let the animal lie down and die. If you pursue it, the animal's adrenalin will increase and cause it to continue to try to escape.

This philosophy is opposed by the thought that if the animal is barely hit, you might miss a second shot and lose it that way. I opted to sit for a few minutes. I sat down on a frost covered log. I didn't smoke cigarettes, so I had a piece of candy. In a few seconds I felt a wetness in my pants from having the warmth of my posterior melt the frost. So much for sitting down and waiting on a frost covered log. I arose and then I heard the sound. A loud groaning and a crash as the animal fell to the ground. I ran over and entered the timber. I found the bull a few yards from the opening. A beautiful 5 x 5 bull. It was still dark in the timber as I opened the neck to complete the bleeding.

The 5 x 5 bull elk that watched the author as he found his missing glove, Wyoming, 1963.

I decided to get some help in field dressing the animal. In ten minutes I was back in camp. Terry was sitting there. He had heard the shot and was expecting something. I told him to limp on down the trail and help me dress the animal. He complained and groaned but we both walked back to the bull.

My bull was very accessible. We quartered him and had him in the truck in a couple of hours. At noon Charles came back and told us he was ready and had located a route to within a few hundred yards of his elk. By evening we had them both back in the camp.

We decided that we would leave in the morning. Terry said that he could not walk in his condition. I told him that I might be able to find another bull for him but he said, "No, I don' t want you to kill my elk and remind me of it for the rest of my life." I agreed and we planned to leave early the next morning and head back to Casper.

The next morning was beautiful as the other days had been. Indian Summer, my most favorite time of the year. We were packed and moving off the mountain by 9:00. Although this had been a great hunt, I suddenly felt an unexplained flush of depression. What's wrong with me? Then I realized that with my finishing school and all the changes in my life, I would probably never come here again.

Terry and Charles bantered all the way down the mountain, as Charles would go through the gyrations necessary on all right hand curves. I didn't say much but my feelings were intensified as we crossed that wood bridge. Tears came to my eyes. There were no vehicles at the ranch. Then I remembered, this was a sharp curve to the right. Charles didn't worry about it he just drove over the sagebrush and pulled upon the highway from the ditch bank. I was glad there wouldn't be any sharp curves between there and Casper.

I have kept in touch with Terry through all of these years. He was successful in developing a large publication company and retired a few years ago. He and his wife attended my 40th Wedding Anniversary in 1994. In fact, I received an e-mail from him today.

Charles was not so fortunate. I lived in Bryan, Texas from 1967-1972. In 1969, I received word that he was in Houston, Texas at the M.D.

Anderson Cancer Institute. (Our name for that hospital was "Marlboro Country," after the popular cigarette). I drove down to visit him one evening with a friend.

He was pleasant and continued to have his grin. He didn't look ill but said that he was receiving treatment for leukemia. We talked about old times for a few minutes. Charles and I were apprentices at the *Casper Morning Star*. I worked closely with him for a couple of years before I left. I reminded him of our elk hunt when he "didn't know if he wanted to hunt rocks or elk." He laughed but didn't respond. I said goodbye and departed. A few months later I received word that he had died in Casper.

The Duckery

The satisfaction of hunting varies with the animal or bird being pursued. All hunting has been enjoyable to me. You cannot compare pheasant hunting with elk hunting. They are just different. This philosophy is analogous to someone trying to compare two beautiful women. One may be a blonde, one may be a brunette. Don't compare, just enjoy them both.

In the mid 1950s I became a friend of Russell "Russ" Madsen. We were both living in Casper. Russ was a geologist for Shell Oil Company. We didn't have much in common, other than hunting. Russ was kind, patient, compassionate and well educated. I was young, brash, impatient and impetuous. However, we made good companions for hunting. We hunted many times for different game.

One day, in October of 1957, we decided to go duck hunting on the opening day out on Horse Creek. This was a very small creek about 65 miles west of Casper. There are probably 15 different Horse Creeks in Wyoming but this is the one we hunted. The creek was very narrow, from 3 to 10 feet wide, making S-turns and meandering through natural grass pastures. Hunting this creek was called "jump shooting." Of course, there are many other ways to hunt ducks, but this was the only way to hunt them on such a creek. We would slip and slink along the creek from bend to bend. As the ducks arose, you shot them, or tried to shoot them, as our skills dictated.

The road followed the creek for several miles. We would hunt separately. We called our method "leap frogging." One would get out and begin to hunt. The other would drive the vehicle about a mile down the creek and park it. When the first hunter got to the vehicle, he would drive a mile above where the other hunter was and park. This way we never had to walk *back to the vehicle.* I thought this was clever but others didn't seem too impressed. Of course, they didn't have to do the walking.

In those days, the opening day of the season did not begin until 12:00 noon. The G&F Department seemed to think that this was more sporting than allowing hunters to start at daylight, as is done on all of the other days of the season. In reality, there would be more ducks on the creek at noon, resting and preening, than at daylight when they would be off searching for food or on larger bodies of water where they would be more protected. I thought about discussing this policy with the G&F biologists. Have you ever tried using logic with a G&F biologist or warden?

This year, the daily limit for ducks was 25, with no restrictions on gender or species. However, on Horse Creek there were mostly Mallards with an occasional Teal, both blue and green wing. I seldom shot Teal. They were pretty small and too difficult to dress for cooking. Russ and I arrived at 11:00 and immediately began a discussion on who would hunt the first section of the creek. My personal opinion was that the second section of the creek would be better, so I politely suggested that Russ take the first section. He did and we began our hunt at exactly 12:00. It probably didn't matter when we started. The nearest warden would be in Casper, 65 miles away, in the local coffee shop.

What a day that was! Warm, pleasant, and no wind. I slipped down to where I thought the first bend would be. There was natural grass about two feet high in places. This often camouflaged the pools and bends well. I mis-judged the distance and two Mallard drakes, quacked behind me as I looked in the wrong direction. Well, I would solve that problem.

I would crawl in the grass from now on. I slithered to the next bend, stood up and four Mallards arose, three hens and a drake. The drakes are so beautiful, with their brassy green necks. For me, they always become the first target. Bang, the drake dropped, bang, bang, and one of the remaining hens dropped in the grass. One advantage of hunting a creek in this manner is that few birds are lost and a dog is not needed. Later, I would use several dogs but at this time I hunted "solo."

As I continued on my first leg of the hunt, I heard Russ shooting constantly. Then I began to wonder, "Should I have taken the first section?" But the ducks appeared to be everywhere along that creek. We were both having a great afternoon. I sure did appreciate the 12:00 noon opening. We each "leap frogged" twice and by then the sun was behind the hills and it was 5:00. I came upon the car and drove up the creek and picked up Russ. We counted 33 ducks, mostly drakes, but with a few hens. Not bad for a half-day hunt.

Russ and I hunted ducks several times during those years. One year we used Russ's canoe and put in at a famous landmark called Devil's Gate on the Sweetwater River, west of Casper, near Independence Rock. The river was low but we floated for several miles. We had a great day. It is much more difficult to hunt in this manner. You have to shoot from a moving canoe and the ducks spook at greater distances. Those ducks were "local" ducks, i.e., they were reared in the area and didn't migrate, and during some winters, they had a difficult time surviving.

Occasionally, we would shoot a northern Mallard. That was a time for celebration. Northern Mallards were much different: deep orange beaks, legs and feet; and they were fat. Local Mallards were thin, more streamlined and their beaks, legs and feet were a pale yellow. The reason for this was the availability of feed. In the areas where we hunted, little grain was raised, and grain was what made a fat duck or any game animal, for that matter.

One day we were looking below Horse Creek and noticed a tree lined pond. There were several flocks of ducks moving and drifting across the small pond, perhaps three acres in size. I said: "Russ, I bet those are northern ducks on that pond. Why don't we come back tomorrow, early, and jump that pond? We can probably sneak up behind the earth dam and be in range." It didn't take Russ long to agree to return the next morning, early.

It was totally dark as we worked our way down, what might be called a road, to near the pond. It was quiet, no moon and it would be 30 minutes or more before light enough to shoot. We laughed as we tried to find our way in the dark, falling over sagebrush with an occasional brush with a coyote hole. I said: "Russ, why are we doing this? We could be home, comfortably in bed." He didn't respond. I have asked several hunting companions that same question. Some day, I'll find the answer.

We sneaked up behind the earth dam. It was about 12 feet high and made good cover. The ducks could not see us. As the light increased, we could hear the ducks on the pond with their incessant quacking, and fluttering noises. We found a spot on the dam with some sagebrush cover. We slowly rose up and looked. There were two flocks of ducks. However, they were clear across the reservoir, way out of range. This was a disappointment. Then I looked and told Russ: "I think they are moving and circling around the pond, Let's just wait and when they come by, we'll blast them." He agreed that this was a good idea.

Every few minutes we would look to see the movement of the ducks. They were feeding, cavorting and having a great time. Occasionally, a duck would stretch up high and flap its wings violently, while giving loud quacks. The sun was beginning to show and the light was much better. As I looked, the two flocks appeared to be different. I recognized the quacks and the sound of the Mallards, but I had no idea what species made up the other flock. I asked Russ, who was beginning to get impatient, which flock to shoot. "The first one that comes by," he retorted.

The wind began to pick up from the southwest and a few ripples began to appear on the pond. The ducks slowly began drifting to the southwest side of the pond, into the wind. Strange behavior I thought. Then, suddenly one flock began to drift directly toward the earth dam, letting the wind help them in the movement. "Get ready. We'll raise up at the same time and shoot them as they begin their ascent," I whispered to Russ.

We each rose up and shot three times. Ducks began falling in every direction. The other flock took off immediately and had soon gained elevation and was heading north toward Horse Creek. We stood up on the dam and looked at the results, six ducks down and dead, one wounded duck swimming toward the other end of the pond. In all of our planning, we didn't think about how we would get them out of the water, if we could hit them. I said: "They'll drift into shore." Russ, now recognizing our mistake said: "Today?"

The wind was still blowing but for fifty yards out from the dam, there was a calm spot. I thought about wading and getting them. The water was deep next to the dam. Suddenly, from behind us, a pickup was approaching. "Oh, I thought, here comes the owner of the reservoir."

The driver got out, went to the back of the truck and let out a big Black Labrador Retriever, which promptly came up and gave us a thorough examination.

The owner of the dog approached us and said: "Having any luck?" We said "yes," and pointed to the carnage in the water in front of us. Within a few minutes that dog had retrieved every duck As we looked at the ducks, we didn't recognize the species. There wasn't much difference in color between genders. Russ and I decided that they were Redheads. I had never shot a Redhead. They were large, almost as big as a Mallard but their shapes were different. We were delighted at our discovery and the work of the dog.

We thanked the owner and asked him if he wanted any of the ducks. He refused our offer. This was many years before the serous decline in duck populations. For several years after, Redheads were almost totally protected. In some flyways one Redhead was 100 points, which was a hunter's daily limit. This part of Wyoming was not in the normal flyway of a Redhead, but for some reason, that small flock decided to rest on that pond so many years ago.

The Floppy-Eared Buck

The 1950's were glorious years for hunting. Plenty of game, fewer restrictions and cheap licenses. Landowners were usually friendly and the population in Wyoming had little growth. We started hunting in late August for sage chickens; elk in early September; antelope in late September; mule deer in October; ducks in October; pheasants in November; rabbits and bobcats the rest of the winter.

In October, 1957, Russ Madsen and I decided that we needed to go deer hunting. I had hunted in several locations across the state, but we thought about hunting north of Casper, out of Kaycee. I didn't know the country well, but had hunted pheasants up there and often spooked deer in the sagebrush draws, as I walked them.

Russ offered to take his 1954 Chevrolet sedan. It was similar to my 1953 Chevrolet coupe. However, my coupe had a larger trunk. We used our cars for hunting. Most of us couldn't afford a pickup and a car. Hunting, in those days, was a lot more work than now. I think back and realize that we were truly "roughing it," without 4 x 4 Pickups, 4-wheelers and snowmobiles.

I knew a few roads southwest of Kaycee. We left Casper early but by the time we arrived at Kaycee and turned towards the Big Horn Mountains, the sun was up. West of this small, mountain town was an abandoned community called Barnum. Apparently, there had been some kind of town there years before. However, by 1957, everything was gone except a community building used for dances and other social activities.

Barnum was kind of a crossroads for going west, south and north. Most hunters went west, high into the Big Horn Mountains. We saw a few cars and trucks with hunters going in that direction. Russ pulled off the main road and stopped at the building, then we continued north on a seldomly used trail. The Pinyon Pine-Cedar breaks began there, with a seemingly endless series of low ridges running north and south.

This was the opening day of the season. We had a good view of the country west as we sat in the truck. "Let's hunt here," I said. For some reason, I didn't want to go high into timber to hunt deer. Russ said that he would hunt a few ridges south and I would hunt a few ridges north. Each ridge was about a half mile long, with a steep draw between. Our plan to hunt a few ridges each was soon changed as we realized the time and energy it took to hike down and back a single ridge.

I stood on the first ridge but decided that I would walk a mile or so north to another ridge. That one didn't appeal to me so I continued north and looked at the third ridge. It had more cover, but had more shelves and shale slopes. I started down the north side, working in a westerly direction. It was dry and noisy and I avoided trees and large rocks. I would occasionally look ahead and across the canyon.

The sun was much higher now and the canyon was well lighted clear to the bottom. I had not heard or seen a thing. I continued downward and then rested for a minute. I thought I saw a deer across the canyon. I looked again and it was a large animal but if it had antlers, they blended into the color of the brush and I couldn't make out if it was a doe or a buck. We both stood motionless. Finally, it moved slightly and the angle changed. It was a buck, a huge buck. I carefully scoped it. It had an incredibly wide rack, but the head looked strange. Something about the head.

Then I noticed that its ears were hanging down in a strange fashion. It moved again and turned more toward me. Where should I shoot it? I estimated it to be 150 yards, not a bad shot. A frontal shot in the chest is deadly. There was nothing around for a gun rest. I would have to shoot off-hand. I squeezed the trigger. The sound of the shot reverberated across the canyon walls. The buck reared up slightly, but then started up the side of the canyon, in huge bounds.

He began to move directly away and then turned at a slight angle. I could see his jaw hanging down. I had missed the chest and hit him in the jaw. He might run for miles without a mortal wound. I scrambled down into the bottom of the canyon and then started up the side. When I reached the top, I looked for his tracks. I could not find any. I was out of breath and slightly faint from the exertion. I began to panic. In what direction did he go after going over the top? I walked a few yards north and south. The ground was hard, with course shale everywhere. I glanced in every direction. Then, I noticed some blood, in blotches, not regular drops. This could mean a major artery was severed and he might not be able to run far. But in what direction?

I knew that my chances of finding this deer decreased every minute that I wasted. Wounded animals usually go down hill if they can. I looked down both sides of this new ridge. Not a sign. Then I saw him, at the same level, going over the top of the second ridge. He was not going down, he was going directly east. I had new hope. I moved much more slowly now, with determination. I crossed the bottom and started up the steep slope of the other side. I carefully came out on top. I looked down, no sign. There he was again, climbing the slope of the third ridge. He stopped on the skyline. I tried for a snap shot as he went over…the dust flew at his feet. I was three feet low, a very poor shot caused by nervousness.

He was gone again. It was almost 30 minutes later, when I finally topped the final ridge. The slope leading to this ridge was the one that I had walked earlier in the morning. I breathed a sigh. I could see nothing in any direction. This was a huge area sloping east down to the road that led to the old community building. It was covered by very tall sagebrush that could hide a herd of deer.

I jumped as a voice behind me said: "What are you looking for?" It was Russ standing on a little rise south of me. I quickly said: "I had been chasing a buck over three ridges. Have you seen him?" Russ smiled and pointed down into a little draw. "He's right down there, about a 100 yards in front of you." I said: "How do you know?" Russ responded: "I saw him go down there and he hasn't come out. I've been watching very carefully. I thought you would eventually come over the hill."

I rested for a few minutes and then slowly began to work my way through the high sagebrush. Russ stayed higher to watch. I had gone about 150 yards, when the buck erupted just a few yards ahead of me. He looked gigantic from the rear. I put the cross hair behind his head and quickly pulled the trigger. He tumbled into the sagebrush. Russ ran quickly over and we examined him.

A huge, old, mature buck. His teeth were badly worn. But he had the strength, after being shot, to lead me on a merry chase. I looked at his large antlers. The mystery of the ears unfolded. The antlers grew straight out for about six inches, instead of up, like most do. This prevented him from holding his ears in the normal fashion. He was my **floppy-eared buck.** This was the largest buck I had killed. It measured a 32-inch spread. However, it did not count well by Boone and Crocket standards. The width of the antlers cannot exceed the length of each beam. Points were deducted. But who cares about points? He was my trophy buck!

The 5 x 5 mule deer buck that led the author on a chase over several ridges. Note the floppy ears and the wounded jaw, Wyoming, 1957.

We were a long ways from the car. Russ and I field dressed him, took some photos and began the long, difficult job of pulling him, whole, through the sagebrush to the car. It took the rest of the day. We were through by 5:00. We were both tired and our hands were sore from hanging on to the antlers as we pulled. I felt sorry that Russ had to spend the rest of the day helping me get the deer out. But he didn't complain. I have already explained to you that he was a kind, patient, compassionate person.

Give Me a .30-06 Dog

No book on hunting could be complete without a general discussion on dogs. I have had several dogs through the years. This discussion will be limited to hunting dogs which are a lot different from general mutts. However, some hunting dogs also serve as pets. General mutts can be lovable pets but most cannot hunt. As a matter of fact, I just watched one neighbor's mutt appropriate another neighbor's property and is rapidly disposing of it on the front lawn.

The hunting dogs that I have owned were: one Weimaraner, one English Pointer, one English Springer Spaniel and four Labradors; two yellow and two black. **The Labrador Retriever is the .30-06 of dogs**, i.e., if you can only have one dog, like only having one gun, for all purposes, the Labrador is one to own. Of course, some people can love and bond with any dog. This fact has always amazed me. The bonding between people and dogs cannot be explained. I have had dogs that I loved as family members. Other dogs I have considered as bastard step-children.

Shortly after Barbara and I married, I purchased a Weimararner Pointer. Some dogs are pointers and some are flushers. I acquired this dog after having had to divorce myself from a couple of generic mutts. In the early 1950's, the Weimararner was the hunting dog of choice around Casper. I had to have one.

My brother-in-law, Von Coles, also had to have one of the new dogs. Actually, they were not new. They had been bred in Germany years before. The news just hadn't arrived in Wyoming until the 1950's. We both hunted with them. One day Von went out to Alcova Lake for some water sports. They had just purchased a new Volkswagen and took it on the trip. They left their dog in the car for a couple of hours. When they returned it had eaten the upholstery in both the front and back seats. When I learned of this I told Von that it wasn't the dog's fault and it served him right for buying a Volkswagen. Von's female Weimararner was ugly but mine had the classic look of the breed.

I was very inexperienced when I first started hunting with this dog, whose name was Bun. I trained him for basic obedience and he was quite cooperative. But he was still a pup and he often tried my patience.

I had a 12-foot kennel on the side of my house, The kennel was right next to the basement entrance of my neighbor on the south. The neighbors were nice people, but the wife was a little prudish. One day, Bun found one of my dress socks, the stretchy kind that was popular in those days. He ate the sock. I didn't miss the sock at the time.

I was out in the kennel one morning. I noticed that Bun was trying to pass that sock, but the stretchy fabric was making this difficult for him. I didn't know what to do. I felt sorry for the dog. I thought about grabbing it and pulling it out but I was afraid, if pain was involved, Bun might bite me. Then I got an idea. If I could make the dog sit down, I could take a stick, push down on the sock, tell the dog to get up and everything would take care of itself.

I called the dog over, had it sit down, and pushed down with the stick. About this time the neighbor woman came out the door and looked over at me and asked me what I was doing. I didn't know what to say, so I didn't respond. Then I thought: "Bun, you and I are in this together." I said: "Heel, Bun." He immediately got up, the sock stretched out about 18 inches and snapped out. The dog let out a yelp and ran to the other side of the kennel. The neighbor looked at me and then the dog and then stick and then the sock, abruptly turned around and walked in the house. She never acted very friendly after that. And that wasn't all, the sock never fit right, either.

Above, the sock eating Weimaraner, Wyoming, 1957. Below, a true .30-06 dog, Kansas, 1978.

Weimaraners were nervous but they were good pointers. I remember the first time I took Bun hunting for ducks out on Horse Creek. It was early one morning. Bun had never seen a duck before. We were quietly slipping along the creek. We came upon a bend and on the far side was one Mallard drake. We were about 20 yards from the bird. I looked down and old Bun was on point. The duck then saw us, took flight and I shot it. It had fallen to the ground. I looked down again and Bun was still on point. He looked like he had rigormortis. My first thought was to look for his off button. But by then, he loosened up and went out and retrieved that duck.

One fall, a friend at work and his son invited me to go turkey hunting. I had never hunted turkeys before. At this time turkeys were not nearly as prevalent as they are today. In fact, they not been introduced or re-introduced in most places, as they have been in the last 20 years. I asked where we could go. About the only place to hunt them was in northeast Wyoming, near Devil's Tower National Monument. We made our plans for a Saturday, a holiday off for all of us.

I decided to take Bun, in case we needed a good pointer. Making this decision should indicate what little I knew about turkey hunting. We arrived early in the morning and immediately began driving around the area. We were never out of sight of the tower and that made the trip special to me. That whole country was spectacular for its fall color.

The area was heavily wooded with a few operating farms and ranches. There were a lot of abandoned homesteads, mixed in with public land. We drove for several hours and never saw a single turkey. We came around this bend and into the yard of a farm. I looked on the far side of the barn and there was a flock of turkeys moving about, feeding. There were a couple of white birds mixed in with the natural colored birds.

I pulled forward, looking for a place to turn around and not disturb the owners. Suddenly I looked at the house and other buildings. They were abandoned...those were wild turkeys! What about the white ones? No answer. We all agreed that they were wild turkeys. I said: "What are we waiting for?" We all jumped out and so did Bun to join us in our pursuit of my first flock of wild turkeys. Our noise spooked the turkeys and they disappeared down a draw.

One hunter ran down one side and I and the other hunter and Bun ran down a fence line. I didn't know what to expect. I knew turkeys could really run fast. They must not have been very frightened. In a few hundred yards we caught up with them across the fence. Gobble, gobble, bang, bang. I didn't realize how big and how noisy several turkeys could be. They are a huge bird. After the dust, powder and feathers settled down, it appeared that we had dropped two out of the flock.

The far one was still flopping. The one in front of me was dead. I started to climb the barbed wire fence but then decided to find out what Bun would do in such a situation. I said: "Fetch, Bun." He rushed under the bottom wire of the fence and was on the bird in a minute. Now Bun had retrieved a lot of birds, but not like this one. He walked around it a couple of times, nosed it and then looked at me. "Fetch. Bun." I said again.

Bun tried to pick up the bird like any other bird. He could not get his mouth around the bird. He nosed it over and looked at me. Then he grabbed it by the neck and began to pull it, backwards toward me. He pulled and shuffled until he reached the fence. I wondered how he would get it through the fence but I decided he had done well enough and I reached down and picked up the large bird.

I hunted pheasants with him several times and he made each hunt much more successful than it would have been without him. In 1961, we moved to Colorado and I had to give him to a friend. I told my friend that he was a good dog but not to leave any socks lying around.

I purchased my first Labrador when we lived in Arizona. Mark was four years old and I thought that they would make good buddies. They did. They were together all of the time for a couple of years. One time Mark wandered off down the creek, near our house, and got lost. The dog never left his side until Barbara found them both sitting under a tree. Mark had been very frightened, but I am sure the dog gave him some comfort.

I cannot tolerate a dog that has not been trained. Life is too short to be burdened by the antics of an untrained dog. This first Lab was named Kernel. He was trained well in basic obedience. However, I never hunted with him. There wasn't anything around that desert area that could be hunted with a retriever. In 1967, we left Sedona and moved to Bryan, Texas. I didn't want to take the dog with me. I just assumed that we would leave the dog. Of all of the mistakes that I made as a father, this stands out in my mind. Thirty years later, Mark told me how hurt he was when we left the dog behind. How I wish that I could go back and remove the pain that Mark must have felt.

My first Black Labrador was named Kate. I bought her in a little town in the middle of Kansas, called Hillsboro. She was a lovable female. I bonded more with that dog than all of the others combined. I brought her home to the boys and we built her kennel. We all worked on the concrete floor and the dog house. We helped her have a litter of puppies. We all felt the loss as each pup disappeared as it was sold. I purchased a book titled *How to Train Your Labrador in 10 Minutes a Day*. That was a great book and I did train Kate in 10 minutes a day. I was extremely busy in those days.

We hunted pheasants constantly. The season lasted three months and we became great companions. She was obedient in the field unless the pheasants started running down a trail or a creek bank and then there was no way I could hold her back. One day we were hunting along a creek. The cover was heavy but a trail went through the cover. She caught the spoor of a pheasant and realized there were several ahead.

She took off and soon pheasants were flushing on all sides of her, mostly roosters, but several hens. She had spooked every pheasant around. I could have slowly beat her to death. Instead I scolded her as I had done several times for the same behavior.

There was a little triangle of cover that she didn't go through. I began to walk through this area, when, right at my feet, a rooster flushed. It swung high to my right over a plowed field. I pulled up and dropped it with one shot. It sailed out about 60 yards. As the dog moved to retrieve this bird, a second rooster got up from the same place. Its flight was exactly the same as the first. I dropped it with one shot. It landed between me and the first rooster.

Kate was trained to always retrieve the birds in order of their being shot, especially ducks. She saw the second pheasant go down and was soon on it. She looked at me and then the pheasant. It was still kicking. She picked it up, gave it a solid bite, dropped it, ran to the first pheasant shot, picked it up, came back and dropped it in may hand. She then returned for the last pheasant shot, picked it up and returned it to my hand. I highly praised her but I also told her that I was still angry about her flushing all of the birds a few minutes before.

In 1978 we moved to the country and Kate came with us. We built her a new kennel and she was right at home. We continued to hunt and have a great time. However, the boys had grown up and she and I were now alone. One day in the fall of 1983, she and I were out for a walk. She was running ahead of me and suddenly she collapsed. I ran to her. She looked at me and tried to get up but collapsed again. I picked her up and took her to her kennel.

My former neighbor had been a veterinarian, and we knew each other well. I took her for an examination. The vet told me she had heart worms and that there was no hope for her. She could not be treated. He said that she would get worse and soon not have enough energy to do anything. In a few weeks she became weaker. I called the vet one day and told him it was time for her to leave. I hugged her for the last time.

I cried all afternoon over that dog. I cried more for her than I have for some people that I have known. I buried her in a special place with her choke collar and identification attached to her marker.

Heart worms were common when I lived in the south. But, it was the general opinion that the disease had not moved into the north or even to the mid west. I could have treated her and saved her life. After that experience, I treated all my dogs and suggested to other dog owners to give the life saving drugs to their dogs. Kate was the only dog that I can remember bonding with. I have owned several other dogs. They were hunting companions but not buddies. Perhaps the loss of Kate seared my feelings or desires to ever get close to another dog.

I have had two other Labrador retrievers. After Kate died I tried having a mutt around the place for a few weeks but disposed of it. Then I found a hunter who had to get rid of a trained 6-year-old female, named Princess. I bought her and took her home. By now I had a business in Randolph, Kansas. I kept her at my plant. She was solid as a hunter and friend.

We hunted a lot and she was loyal and kind. But I never bonded as I had done in the past. I began to notice that she couldn't see well and then she became absent minded. It was evident that she was in a rapid decline. I could not hunt with her and I hated to see her stagger around. I took her to the veterinarian. I said goodbye to her, gave her a pat and left the office before others could see my tears. But my grief was short lived as I was not as emotionally attached as I was with Kate.

I wanted to hunt pheasants and a dog is needed for serious hunters. I heard about a breeder out of Wichita that had trained dogs for sale. I called and he said he had one about ready. I drove down to Herrington, Kansas to see this dog. The trainer was honest. He said: "I don't like this dog. She is too exuberant, too hard to handle, too intense. She is not worth what my other dogs are. I'll sell her to you for $600." Well, the normal price was $2500, so the price was right. But if a trainer had problems what chance would I have? The trainer took her out and she worked magnificently. I was impressed. I bought her.

Her nickname was Suds, taken from her registered name Cheyenne Mountain Light. The owner must have been impressed by beer commercials. She only had two speeds, high and stop. That was the most intensely motivated dog I had ever seen. Her only purpose in life and passion was retrieving. I continued to train her and she was a super retriever. I watched her turn a somersault, one day in the mud, turning on the scent of bird. Her eye marking of downed birds was sloppy. She knew her nose would take care of any mistake in distance. We hunted a lot, but in those years, birds were usually scarce so we didn't get near the birds that Kate and I had bagged.

One afternoon, in January, we went pheasant hunting a few miles west of Randolph, Kansas. We stopped at a bridge to begin our hunt. The birds were wild and running and so was Suds. I was having a hard time holding her in. Late in the afternoon, she disappeared. I couldn't find her. I finally went back home without her. The first time I had ever lost a dog. (I didn't count the English pointer, discussed later). She was wearing her I.D., so I knew any honest person would call me upon finding her.

Three days later I got a call. A farmer said that this dog had been staying under that bridge for three days. Suds had returned to the place where we started, looking for me and would not leave. The farmer finally caught her and called me. She was pleased to be back home in her kennel. When I retired, I could not bring two dogs to Utah so I sold her to an avid duck hunter. I never heard from him. I hope that she is well treated and doing a lot of hunting. I never really bonded with her so when she jumped into the her new owner's pickup, I was unmoved.

When we first arrived in Kansas in 1972, I needed a dog for pheasant hunting. I looked around and found a kennel. I thought that buying an older, well trained dog would save all of the hassles of training my own. I had been around English Pointers. A well trained pointer is a delight to observe. The kennel owner had a three-year-old English Pointer for sale. He told me she was trained and that her owner had to move and couldn't take her with him. I could understand that situation. I asked the boys if they wanted her and they said yes.

We kept her in a kennel for a couple of weeks. It was September and the dove season had opened. The boys were small and I thought it would be fun to have them go with me and watch the action as I tried to hit those fast moving targets. I asked around and found that a good place to hunt was on a Christmas tree farm near where a friend lived. We arrived in good spirits. I told the boys the dog was not a dove dog but it would be good for all of us to watch her work. I let her out and she started down the first row of trees, moving south. As far as I know she is still running. I never saw her again. The boys couldn't understand why she didn't come back and I couldn't tell them. I often wonder how many times the kennel owner had sold that dog.

In 1995, Suds was as active as ever, providing non-stop agitation to me. She was so hyper that it was difficult to let her out to see the grandkids. She would be so enthusiastic in seeing them she would run up and knock them down. I thought that I would like to have another dog of a different breed. My grandson, Matthew had an English Springer Spaniel and a Gordon Setter. This was a strange combination of dogs. I liked the spaniel but the setter was not only weird looking but weird acting. The setter's name was Gruder. I named him "Grody." The spaniel's name was Cassie. That dog must have had a strange diet. I named him "Gassie," for obvious reasons.

I noticed an ad in the paper for Springer Spaniel pups in Council Grove, Kansas. I drove down there and bought a new pup and named her Blaze. When my oldest son, Mark, heard that I had a Springer Spaniel, he said: "Dad's personality is not going to match with that dog's personality." This proved to be a prophetic statement.

I enjoyed Blaze in many ways. I trained her well and she impressed all who would watch her being put through her paces. However, she had a will of her own and most activities were done *on her terms*. Such is the nature of a Springer. They are similar to Cocker Spaniels in that way. I trained her to retrieve well, but if for some reason she did not want to retrieve, she didn't. Or, if she decided to go eat the Capok trainer, she would do that. I took her bird hunting several times. She would retrieve them if she felt like it. Her nose was very poor. I have watched her step over a pheasant in a bush and not know it.

She helped me develop more patience for dogs than I had before. However, she would turn on me if provoked and I could never get over that. She was perfectly house-broken in my shop for years. Then she decided she would relieve herself where and when she pleased. I was bringing her to Utah from Kansas. We stopped at a motel one cold, stormy night in North Platte, Nebraska.

I didn't want to leave her in the truck or in her kennel outside because it was so cold. So I took her into the motel. I was unloading the gear and settling down. She climbed up on the bed that I was to sleep on. I told her to get off the bed. She refused. I took her collar and started to pull her off the bed. She bit me. She turned on me on several other times. I sold her to a private game farm. I thought that she would like all of the hunting she would get to do with the clients.

A young man bought her. He was impressed with her and wanted to train her to "be his dog." I thought she would respond well to a lot of personal attention. About three months after she left, I received a call from the man, Dustin. He said she was not working out and that he didn't want her. She wouldn't hunt and would pout most of the time. If there were other dogs around she would bite them. If she was corrected in any way, she would pout. I was disappointed. I didn't want that dog back. However, I promised him that I would take her back if she didn't work out.

I went to get her. She immediately recognized me but wasn't overly friendly. I brought her home and put her in my shop where she has lived for four years. She appeared a little miffed, walked into the shop and relieved herself. I tried to make up with her but she continued to be aloof. She acted strange. The next day she ate my shop door. **Give me a .30-06 dog!**

Half-Price Sale

I had always wondered how I got on the mailing lists for obscure products and services. Most of the literature was immediately trashed. So many trees were sacrificed for such little benefit.

However, one day in early May in 1991, I received a package with a huge Rainbow Trout on the guide and outfitter's logo. This was from The Alaska Rainbow Lodge, touted as the "Premier fishing lodge in Alaska." This was "high dollar" printing and layout. Inside was a "personal" letter to me telling me about the lodge, the super fishing and all of the other normal propaganda. I read on. The 4-star lodge accommodated 12 guests. The lodge opened the third week of May.

Then a special paragraph caught my attention. A prominent doctor had booked the whole lodge for the second week of June. He had become ill and had cancelled his reservation. Therefore, at this late date, if I was one of the first 12 to call, I could come up at **half-price.**

Most people jump at anything that reeks of a sale. I, on the other hand, being the skeptic that I am, carefully look for the bait-and-switch scam. A lifetime of being "baited" has produced this character flaw. The literature on this lodge looked like a college catalog. I called the 800 number and visited with the owner and outfitter's wife for 30 minutes discussing all of the intricacies of such a trip. Now, this woman was a sales person. I asked her where her husband was and she responded that he was already in Alaska preparing for this year's fishing season.

I had fished the general area several years before. But that was a huge area and I was not familiar the river the lodge was on. But I trusted that the lodge did, in fact, exist. A little experience in Alaska warns one to be cautious of the dishonest guides and outfitters. I still had not forgotten Rene Limmeres. The second week of June was a little early for King Salmon fishing. I asked her what fish that would be available at that time.

She was knowledgeable and listed them: Grayling, Dollie Varden, Rainbows, Arctic Char and Pike. I had caught them all in reasonable quantities, except Pike. However, for such a trip, I wanted to catch Salmon, as I had for every other trip to Alaska. I checked their fish calendar and noticed they would be fishing for King Salmon the following week. I said: "I will book with you if you promise to take me King Salmon fishing the last day of my week." "No problem," she said. I thought for a minute where I had heard that before...Oh, Andy Sidewinder, from Montana, had said that to me.

I didn't have much time to plan for this trip. However, I began to make my extensive list. The first thing on the list was my neoprene chest waders and then, of course, all of the other things. Mark had made me a special light rod that would be perfect for this trip. He had made me a medium weight rod years before and I loved that rod.

The rod was beautiful, the result of good workmanship. Part of its value was that it was made by my son. The literature stated that "A well-stocked fishing gear store was located at the lodge." I was pleased as I made sure that I had everything that I could possibly use for a week packed in my bag.

The day of departure finally came. I would be flying out in the evening and arrive at Anchorage before midnight. Anchorage was three hours earlier than Kansas. On the way down, I stopped to visit a good friend of mine, Don Schulz, who was in a rehabilitation hospital, recovering from a stroke. As we visited, how thankful I was for my good health. Don and I were the same age. Don was not a fisherman. I wondered if that had anything to do with the fact that he had a stroke.

The non-stop Northwest Airlines Plane was only a third full, which made the trip more pleasant. I, and my gear arrived safely. This had not always been the case in the past. I stayed at the International Hotel. I did not sleep well. A guest, right above me, insisted on beating his female companion most of the night. I called the night clerk several times but without success. The next morning, I kept looking for a battered woman but never did see one.

The new day was beautiful, bright and sunny. Anchorage and the whole of Alaska was cloudy much of the time. It certainly was not like mid-America, where I was coming from. I often thought that Alaska was a *feeling as well as a place*. This usually came at about the time the plane was descending above Cook Inlet. Our flight to King Salmon was wonderful. I met two guests who were going to the Alaska Rainbow Lodge with me.

A lodge pilot met us at the airport and transported us to the bay where we boarded a float plane and flew out to the lodge. The plane was a remodeled and well maintained Beaver, the workhorse of Alaska. The fight only took 30 minutes. The lodge was located on the Kvichak River. This was a large river. It is hard to explain this vast country and its beauty. I will not try. However, it was completely different from the Kanectok River and that whole flood plain area, discussed in the **Is the Gun Loaded?** story.

We landed in the large river and taxied up to the dock. Two other float planes were also tied up at the dock. I looked up and saw a large, western style building, with a large American flag gently blowing in the breeze. What a setting! We were greeted by part of the staff. I found later that the staff ratio was 1:1, which was unusually high.

Since I was by myself, I had a lovely room. It was the finest room I have ever had, in any hotel, in any part of the world that I have stayed. This appeared to be a truly 4-star lodge. The bathroom was beautiful. The towels were so thick and heavy, I could barely pull them off the racks. The carpet throughout was the most expensive type. The kitchen was immaculate. Other floors were tile or linoleum with a high gloss wax finish.

Soon, a staff member came and interviewed me about my eating habits, what I liked to drink, the kinds of booze that I wanted, the type of lunch that I wanted during the day and other relevant information. From then on, those directions were followed and were never mentioned again. I spent the evening getting my gear in order for the week's fishing. Each person or group had a guide and pilot at their discretion. Weather permitting, the species of fish and location were explained and planned.

I met the other guests, mostly high rollers, professional, of course, with a couple of businessmen. During the evening, names were dropped of some of the past clients, like the infamous Charles Keating, of the large savings and loan debacle in Arizona. Now I know what he may have done with some of that $450 million.

There was a bar, lounge and beautiful dining room. Clients could have any kind of liquor they wanted. I stayed with my Dr. Pepper but I was about the only non-drinker in the group. There didn't appear to be any smokers among the guests, which made the living conditions much better.

I was curious about the power supply for such a lodge in the middle of the wilderness. I looked around some of the outbuildings. One building had three 10,000 watt generators in tandem for power. Everything had to be flown in from Anchorage or transferred from King Salmon. There were three deep freezes, and walk-in coolers and all of the other necessary equipment for a first class kitchen.

Meals were a delight, that is, if you didn't mind making decisions. There were choices of at least four entrees and then all of the other dishes. Several desserts were offered. There were chandeliers above the tables. Full, formal table service was offered, with gold plated eating utensils. On the last night of our visit, there was an ice sculpture on the table. This was a first for me!

Staff members were kind and accommodating, with the exception of the Guide-Coordinator, Dean Speer. For some reason, I immediately felt a distrust for him. I mentioned immediately that I was supposed to be taken for King Salmon fishing at the end of the week. He would not commit to any such plan.

Top, the 4-star lodge in the middle of the wilderness. Middle, plenty of float planes for guests. Below, the farewell cake given after the "fisherman roast," Alaska, 1991.

I felt uncomfortably out of place. Not that I couldn't meet the intellectual or social environment but I was there on a fishing trip. What type of person had such vanity that he would need those kinds of trappings? I did understand the business aspect of fulfilling the demand, as a profit making enterprise.

The first day's fishing was rather uneventful. The weather was cloudy so we took large john boats and fished various holes of the river for rainbows. I caught a few that averaged 3-4 pounds. They were fighters. Those Rainbows were not hatchery reared and hybrids; they were called Leopard Rainbows and were self propagating in those wonderful waters.

At first, my guide would try to carry everything for me, change my lures, almost land my fish. I took him aside and informed him that I am capable of doing all of those things for myself. He backed off and we began to have more of a normal fishing experience.

That night, my guide and I met with one of the pilots and we discussed how and where I wanted to fish. I told them that I wanted to go up some of the main rivers, camp out and fish for the three or four species found there. Camping would give me a more normal feeling for fishing and ease my conscience for staying at such a pretentious place. I didn't want to float a river. I was still healing from the Kanectok River experience, some six years before.

One other client wanted to go with me, so the pilot, two guides and two clients made up this party. We would be gone for three days. I didn't understand how they were going to handle all of the logistics, so I watched carefully. We flew out on a float plane, into the sun of a glorious Alaska spring day. We turned and followed a river north-west, until it began to be reduced to a much smaller stream. The plane set down on what appeared to be the last long stretch of calm water.

We all unloaded the plane and put all of the gear on the beach. Both guides disappeared into the brush and came out shortly with two medium sized john boats with jet motors. The plane taxied to the end of the long hole and roared off back to the lodge. The guides told me they had to hide their boats and gear to be safe from all of the natives in the area. They destroyed or removed any of the lodge gear when found.

We had everything that we would need for a great camping trip. We had 1 x 1 guide service. Everything looked super. We moved rapidly up the stream. I had never been able to discern the difference between creek, stream and river. All three of them came in different sizes. And then, in some areas, there was another sort of water resource called "crick." There were a lot of cricks in Wyoming.

In a few miles the terrain became more mountainous and we were moving up in altitude. We slowed at the confluence of another stream about the same size. The guides asked us how that looked. It looked great to me. We could fish either stream. We pulled up each boat to the beach and unloaded the gear. I helped until I came to my fishing gear and then I quit helping, for obvious reasons. There were several great holes within a few hundred yards of our campsite. I asked one of the guides if he had a shotgun for protection. He nodded his head. I then asked if it was loaded. He nodded again. I was greatly relieved.

My fishing buddy and I began to fish the holes. He was a fly fisherman and so I had two or three nice Dolly Varden caught before he was ready. I have been around a lot of fly fishermen, one of whom is my oldest son, Mark. As a spinner and bait fisherman, I learned to be careful about any philosophy discussions. I assumed my new companion was a "catch and release" person. While I sometimes changed from "catch and release," to "hook and cook."

Our guides had all of the tents up and prepared. We had two sleeping tents and an eating and lounging tent. They were laughing and having a good time. I was beginning to like this style of fishing and camping safari. I thought about having them call me "Bwana," but then changed my mind.

We fished, laughed and told stories all afternoon and evening. Now an Alaska evening is about 10 hours that time of the year. At about 11:00 p.m., I was ready for bed and went to the tent and retired even though the sun was still hovering in the west.

During the night my feet got cold and never did warm up. In the morning I looked and there was ice on the water bucket. A heavy frost covered everything outside of the tents. We began another day of successful fishing. The fish were hitting pretty well. By mid-afternoon, I was bored and did a little exploring around the area. I didn't walk too far. I always have bears on my mind. However, I didn't see any sign.

We had dinner that evening. I asked my guide what was up this one stream on the west. He said it got pretty rough up about two miles and eventually reached impassible rapids. He asked me if I would like to go up for a ways. I nodded yes. We could get away by ourselves and see new country.

We took the john boat and started out. We stopped and fished at some of the more inaccessible holes. He was very good at handling the boat. He could hover the boat and I could cast into those neat hiding places for those Rainbows. The fish were getting larger now. Why didn't we come up here earlier? The guide responded that he was saving this for last! I caught two four pounders in a few minutes.

We continued up a mile or so more. The guide stopped where the water was rolling over a big log, with a neat hole on one side. I was using a Mepps spinner. He said cast: "in there." The spinner had barely hit the water when, Wham, and the fight was on. The boat was rocking and the fish suddenly started up stream. I tried to let out my line so we could follow. The line went under the boat and the fish was gone–that fast. I asked: "How big do you think that baby was?" "At least six pounds," the guide responded. I was disappointed. Then the guide said: "Would you like to go up stream where they are *really big?*" I said, "Of course, let's go." Not knowing what might be in store.

Off we roared, moving around logs, rocks and an occasional section of rapids. This went on for several minutes, getting more difficult all of the time. Now and then the guide would have to reverse the boat and move backwards. About this time, I was becoming very nervous as I was violently pitched from side to side. "This is far enough," I yelled at him. He didn't respond. We came around a sharp curve. There ahead was a large rapids pouring down over sheer cliffs. At the foot of the cliff was a huge hole, boiling and then quietly becoming a deep pool.

The trip there was very unpleasant, but what a hole! I told the guide that I wanted to get out and fish from the bank. The problem was, there was almost no bank. He said: "Fish from the boat." But I insisted and then got out and worked my way along the bank to where I could cast into that boiling water.

I changed lures. I wanted a heavier one to sink into the depths of that hole. There was almost no room to cast. Willows came right down to the edge of the water. There was a small shelf and then it dropped right into the deep water. I cast out, missed and hit the rocks. I tried again. Same results. I then cast around from my left side. It worked. The spinner dropped into the hole and disappeared. The current caught it and it was moving in all directions. I reeled to tighten the line. Then, all of a sudden, I felt a violent jerk, the line tightened and the fight was on. The fish moved from the boiling pot to the slower, deeper water. He was moving downstream.

I adjusted the drag on my reel but the 8-pound test line continued to scream out. I tightened it more and the line went limp. I had lost that huge fish! I began to reel in, thinking that I had lost the fish and my lure. Suddenly the line tightened and the fish was moving back into the boiling hole. That fish tried that same tactic three times before he began to tire. I could now turn him a little as I tried to work him to the shore.

Finally, he was within ten feet of the narrow bank. I continued to slowly reel him in. It was difficult to keep my balance, hold the rod high over my head and nurse him ashore. I called to the Guide: "Throw me the net." He yelled back: "I don't have a net." I had to land that fish for a photo. He was within arm's length, I reached for him, but slipped on the shelf and went in to my hips. Fortunately, my chest waders saved me from having that icy water cover me. But in my fright, I dropped my rod. I quickly retrieved it.

I called to the guide, who had been laughing and giving me encouragement until he saw me slip, and then he had started towards me. I looked at him, feeling a sort of frantic helplessness and said: "Come and help me land this fish." The guide, now guffawing loudly said: "I thought you wanted to do everything for yourself." He came over and retrieved the fish and gently placed it in my hands for a photo." The fish was about 28 inches long, with a deep girth and perfectly formed. "How big is it," I asked the Guide. "Oh, about 8 pounds," he responded.

"Don't stop now. There are larger ones in that hole," the Guide encouraged me. I thought for a minute and then walked to the boat. "Where are we, I asked?" He responded: "Just inside the boundary of the Katmai National Monument." I looked at my watch—11:00 p.m. I looked back at that boiling, noisy rapids.

"No, I want to keep this memory. We came clear up here and invaded that fish's home. He is back now and I don't want to disturb that sacred hole again." The Guide nodded and looked at me in a strange sort of way. I climbed into the boat and we started our labored journey back to camp. When we arrived, the others were asleep. I had a bite to eat and retired. I was so tired that I didn't notice my cold feet.

Top, plenty of rainbows in all of the rivers. Middle, guides preparing to meet the float plane. Below, the Leopard Rainbow caught in the sacred hole, Alaska, 1991.

The next day was clear and bright. My fishing companion and I didn't move about with such fervor that day. We had a large breakfast cooked by the Guide. As I ate, I watched the merging of the streams and enjoyed the bird life in the trees nearby. We had seen several Bald Eagles and one was now soaring high above our camp.

I put down my gear and explored the area between the two streams. However, I was nervous about bears, so I didn't go far. I continued to fish for another hour. I caught a few more Dollie Varden but after the experience of the night before, this was not very challenging. I was ready to go back to the lodge.

The Guides broke camp and we all loaded the two boats. Our trip down the stream was uneventful. The float plane was waiting as we approached the hiding place of the boats. We loaded the plane and the Guides spent 30 minutes hiding the boats in a nearby inlet. How sad, I thought to have the natives be destructive. I said a silent prayer that they would not be disturbed. I also, selfishly, said a prayer that the next party would not find my sacred hole.

After a hot shower and the usual gourmet meal, I was ready to discuss the next day's outing. I chose to take the float plane to some hidden lakes near the coast for the same species. However, the main attraction was the incredible natural setting. I was more occupied with looking at the volcanic type mountains, the bears coming and going and responding to the several squalls than I was fishing. We had to sit in the plane while the last squall passed before roaring back to the lodge. I continued to be amazed at the raw engine power necessary to get off the water with floats.

I had one day left. I approached Dean Speer and reminded him of the agreement that I had made to receive one day of King Fishing on the coast. This was not far away and the lodge clients would be fishing there next week. He responded by saying: "I am not going to disrupt my week's plans by taking you King Salmon fishing." I was disappointed and angry. Are there any outfitters who keep their word?

Everyone was nervous the last day. The clients were coming and going everywhere. One plane roared off earlier than the others. I asked where they were going and Dean Speer said: "Pike fishing way up north." I told Speer: "I would have liked to have gone with them. I have never caught Pike in Alaska." Speer just shrugged his shoulders. I took a john boat and fished the river the last day. I caught a few nice Rainbows but I didn't get to go for King Salmon or PiKe.

The last night's meal was special. An ice sculpture appeared on the table, with a choice of entrees, including lobster and prime rib. A special cake was brought in with our names spelled out in vanilla frosting. Then, after the meal, came the special awards. It was more of a roast, than an award ceremony. I received the "Can of Worms Award" for having lost the most lures during the week.

After the awards ceremony, all the clients were gathered together in the dining room. The owner of the lodge, Ron Hayes was sitting in the group. He had been around all week. I only saw him a few times but he did guide one of the other groups a time or two. He was not very talkative, at least to me. I tried to ask him questions about general things but it was evident that he didn't want to communicate.

However, this night it was different. He was much more jovial, brought on, perhaps, by being primed by a little alcohol. We talked fishing. However, in the past, he had been a major hunting guide and outfitter and operated out of this lodge most of the time. He changed the subject to hunting. He had been caught in a major Alaska Wildlife Resources sting operation that was conducted over several years. He was finally indicted and convicted of hunting the same day as flying. This was a major felony.

He was sentenced to a year in prison at Leavenworth, Kansas. I couldn't believe this! Then I remembered a TV documentary that I had watched a few months before. This was the man in the show. I didn't understand serving time in a federal prison for a state crime but I didn't pursue the topic. At this point he became angry and began to vent his feelings. He said it cost him a plane, his hunting outfitter's license for life and around $100,000 legal fees.

This sounded absurd to me. A person can be convicted for manslaughter and not receive that sentence!

    The whole staff met us at the dock and said goodbye. We flew in a float plane back to King Salmon and then to Anchorage and then back to Kansas City. This was the first fishing trip to Alaska when I was not taking fish home to eat. However, I was taking one very special memory of a fish home to be mentally digested forever.

The Idaho Scam

In the spring of 1995, I contracted another serious case of "Hunting Fever." This is not to be confused with "Fishitis," which has already been discussed, but not in detail. Fishitis is an infection and can only be cured by a least one successful fishing trip. It may take several trips before a successful one comes along. But Hunting Fever is, literally, a fever, seldom going over 108 degrees, but none-the-less has to be treated. The treatment is different than Fishitis. A hunting trip of any kind, successful or not, can solve the problem. In fact, a hunting failure can really take that fever down.

My wife, Barbara, knows the symptoms well. Hunting advertisements spread over my desk, maps, and long phone calls, with me whispering at times, especially when prices for anything appeared to be discussed.

This trip was going to be different. In doing our family history research, I had discovered an Uncle, living in Kamiah, Idaho. His name was Bill Karman, my Mother's brother. He was the last living survivor on that whole side of the family.

We had corresponded with his wife for years, but after she died, Bill never wrote. I found out later that he was barely literate. But we had talked to him on the phone. If I could find an outfitter in that part of Idaho, I could combine a hunting trip and see the old man before he died. He was 91 at the time.

I came across an ad in a prominent hunting magazine for an outfitter that could guide: "In Idaho, or Montana, with vast acres of private leases and public land." I have learned that private leases are far superior to public land. Access is limited, successful management can be applied and there is no competition for hunting rights. I began a dialogue on the phone with the owner and manager of the operation. I asked for references. He sent me a few names to call.

I don't understand how the poorest performing, dishonest outfitter can get people from all parts of the country to give glowing reports of the big game hunts. They must pay individuals, like large companies pay celebrities, to lie to the public.

My oldest son, Mark was living in Reno, Nevada. I thought if he wanted to join me, he could meet me in Kamiah, we could visit with Bill and then head north to the Panhandle of Idaho. I chose to hunt in Idaho since the last year I had hunted in Montana with an outfitter named Andy Sidewinder.

Mark agreed to come. I told Bill when we would be by and I began to think about packing. I love to pack. I began this ritual in the early planning stages of any hunt. This habit has been formed by a series of hunting trips and fishing trips where major catastrophes have occurred when needed items had been neglected or left at home.

We had to buy our licenses. In some states, that is a long and arduous process. Some states go through the motions of a lottery system. Others have an open license system. Some permits, if hunting on private land, can by purchased directly from the landowner, or his lessee. However, in Idaho, at that time, a streamlined system was available. Call an 800 number, give your vital statistics, credit card number and the license is in the mail. Of course, out-of-staters have to buy the combo-license, both deer and elk. For this I paid $800 plus a "processing charge."

Mark arrived in Kamiah shortly after I did. We spent the rest of the day visiting or trying to visit with Bill. We stayed in one of the local motels that night. Bill bristled when I told him we were going to go up north to hunt. "I could have taken you right around here," he hissed at me. "I know these mountains but if you want to go up to that part of the state and pay some dude to take you out, that's your business," he continued.

He calmed down after a while and we discussed other subjects. He was a colorful old man. He was a renegade in the family, seldom associated with his brothers or sisters and appeared to have a mean streak in him, somewhat mellowed by living 91 years. He told of his early history in the Army. He had been in the cavalry and had learned to be a farrier. He made his living the rest of his life taking care of horses.

He talked of elk hunting a lot, especially in Colorado, where he used to live before moving to Idaho. He talked of hunting on horses, shooting bulls, missing cows and the general tales of a hunter. He had been in Idaho for about 20 years. He loved the mountains. Kamiah is located in a narrow valley, deep within the mountains of western Idaho. I had assumed that he had been successful in hunting elk in Idaho. However, later, I was visiting with one of his friends, about his age who said: "That old son-**-*-**** hasn't killed an elk in Idaho since he's been here."

Later in the day, we discussed hunting guns, the best calibers for hunting deer and elk and hand guns. He lamented all of the new rules and regulations and said that the country was "going to hell." He said that in his elk hunting days he liked to use a Model 70, Winchester .300 Magnum. I said that I used a .30-06. He was offended. He said that he had a .30-06 but used it only for deer and antelope, but you really needed a .300 Magnum for elk. My memory quickly went back to a time when I was hunting deer with a guy who was using a .300 "Mag." He made a direct hit and when we examined the deer it was shot so well, we couldn't figure out what sex it was. But I wasn't going to argue with old Bill about *anything*.

At about this time, Bill shuffled over to his bed. He lived in a small mobile home by himself. He reached under the mattress and retrieved a Model 70, Winchester .30-06. His eyes began to sparkle as he discussed the hunting history of that gun. I had one just like it, but said nothing. He reached under the mattress again and pulled out 1938 Model 70 Winchester .300 Magnum. It had a scope on it the size of a 4" inch galvanized pipe.

Bill slowly caressed that gun. It showed the marks of having been carried in a scabbard on a horse on many trips. He then showed me the scabbard. It looked as if the rats had been gnawing on it in places, but it was still valuable to Bill. He worked the bolt a couple of times and said: "This is *The Elk Gun.*" He thrust the gun into my hands and said: "Try it." I tried to look interested and asked a couple of questions. Then he said: "I want you to have this gun." I was suddenly moved by his generosity. My own Step-dad never gave me a gun, or anything else, for that matter. I humbly thanked him. He looked down and in an apologetic way said: "I won't be needing it any longer."

We went out to eat that night in the local cafe. I helped Bill order as he tried to read the menu. We said goodby. Mark and I were going to leave early in the morning for Montana.

It was a long drive to Wisdom, Montana, the little town from which the outfitter operated. My newly possessed .300 "Mag" was safely packed in the backseat of my 1994 Ford pickup, converted to propane. (I am embarrassed to say that after 40 years, I would try one more Ford). I had no intention of using that gun on this trip. I wasn't sure I could carry it over a hundred yards. It was several months before I shot it. I now know why they called them magnums...they kill on both ends.

We pulled into this tiny town and asked for directions to the address given me by the outfitter. The building was hard to find, tucked away in a cul-de-sac at the end of a road near the side of a pine covered hill. It was a large building. It looked like a college dorm. I looked in back and there was a shooting range. It had a large parking lot. In it were a few cars, apparently belonging to clients. Then on the other side of the lot was a fleet of Chevrolet suburbans, with the sign and logo of the outfitter. I was impressed. "This is going to be some hunt," I thought.

We were hunting the first week of the season, tomorrow was October 15, the opening day. Mark and I walked into the building. It had a huge lounge, with a large fireplace. It looked like the Smithsonian Museum of Natural History. There were mounts all over the walls of huge elk, deer, bear, moose, mountain lions, etc. My trigger finger itched just looking at them.

The next room was a dining room with tables and benches. Sleeping accommodations appeared to be upstairs. We met the owner and outfitter. He was a large man, but he seemed to have a dark countenance about him. He reminded me of Marlon Brando in *The Godfather*. He was loud and vulgar. Every other word was the F-word. He took the balance of the money owed, checked our licenses, and assigned us to our room. We would have a room to ourselves, although there were four bunks available. The outfitter told us that our guides would meet us that night, to discuss the hunt for tomorrow.

At about 8:00 p.m. most of the clients were gathered in the dining room and the lounge. The door opened and a stream of young men began to enter. Most looked like college students, however, there were three or four that looked like guides, i.e., beards and grubby clothes. In discussing the hunt with the outfitter, one of the attractive conditions was a 1 x 1 hunt. That is the ratio for guides to hunters. That meant that every hunter had his own guide, if desired. Or, if two hunters wanted to be together, one guide would be furnished. That would be 2 x 1. Mark decided that he wanted to hunt by himself. That was okay with me since he had been kind of grouchy on the trip and I didn't want to make him worse by out shooting him.

Everyone paired off, or in some cases, three men had formed their committees. I was impressed. It looked like a sorority party. My guide was a guy about 35 years old, sort of refined, and friendly. He had been going to college, dropped out and was trying to earn enough money to return. He didn't say how many years he had been saving. Mark didn't say much about his guide. My guide began to point to the trophies on the wall and asked me what size of animal I wanted to shoot and got some general information on my hunting background. I couldn't believe this! The guide acted as if we could go out in the morning and select our animal. Was this going to be some kind of a game farm?

I began to gather some statistics. There were 19 clients or hunters in the building. The building could accommodate 24. There were 15 men posing as guides. In addition there was the outfitter, his wife and two other women, a cook and a helper. Through the evening and the next morning, I ascertained that none of the 19 hunters was a repeat client.

Most, with the exception of a couple, had never hunted elk before. Most were from the eastern states, and this appeared to be a grand experience. I was pleased for them, but, for some reason, I had a strange premonition about what was going to happen the following days.

We were told to be up early, breakfast was at 5:15 sharp. I didn't sleep well. The dorm-type rooms and bunk beds reminded me of my military experience and that would keep anyone awake. I was the first one down for breakfast. The outfitter sat at his own private table, a cup of coffee in one hand and a cigarette in the other hand. He watched as each hunter, one by one, came down the stairs. I watched also. None appeared to be over 45 years old, most were professional, a doctor or two, a lawyer and then other mixed occupations. Almost all were over weight. Some were dressed in the latest and most expensive Cabela clothing.

Soon all of the guides came in and the whole room was full, buzzing with simultaneous conversations. The outfitter began to bark out orders to individual guides across the room about areas to hunt and vehicles to use. Of course, the F-word was used liberally whenever considered appropriate. This whole operation was something I had never seen in all of my hunting experiences.

Mark went with his guide and disappeared into one of the suburbans. I, one other hunter, and two guides climbed into a late model, white suburban. Of course, all were 4 x 4, which gave me some feeling of security. We drove about 30 minutes. The guides made arrangements to handle the vehicle. My guide and I got out and started up this, what appeared to be, skid trail. However, in the dark, I had no idea what direction we were going. That was an advantage of having an experienced guide.

We hiked up the first hill at a moderate pace. When it became light enough to see, I looked around the area. We were in a series of very steep, heavily timbered mountains. As the day progressed, we would leave the main trail to hunt side trails and skid trails. Most of the area had been cut over sometime in the past 20 years. This was much different than the Wind River Range, which I was so familiar with. Most of the hiking was up severe slopes. By noon, my feet began to become sore from walking for hours on side hills.

We continued until mid-day. I was becoming very tired. After lunch, we started through a thick patch of Lodgepole Pine. I heard a noise from one side and a cow and a spike spooked in front of me. I threw up my scope but decided that I did not want to shoot a spike and the cow season was not open.

The rest of the day proved unproductive. I saw very little sign and it appeared to me that this was not habitat where elk would spend any time. There appeared to be little feed. I couldn't figure out why we hadn't been hunting on some of the "vast acres of private land," stated in the promotional literature.

By 4:00, I began to wonder if I had enough energy to get back to the vehicle. The guide acted surprised when I told him. I then informed him that I was in my 60's and that I thought this was a hunting trip and not a walking marathon. As we returned to our point of departure, I had to rest more often, until at the last, I was resting about every 10 minutes. My feet were sore but I didn't think I had blisters, which would have ended the hunt. My knees ached from going down the slopes. Hiking up hills is easier on my knees than hiking down hills.

The other guide and hunter were waiting for us to return. That hunter had quit about 2:30 and they had been waiting since that time. He was exhausted and looked flushed to me, from his exertion. He fell asleep as we drove back to the headquarters.

As I walked through the dorm, I saw that everyone had returned. They all looked like a company of boot camp recruits. I talked to one overweight man from Pennsylvania, as he rubbed his bare feet. He said that he was through, he couldn't hunt this way. Another diabetic hunter's blood sugar was off and he had a relapse in the afternoon. I thought, two down and 17 to go.

Mark was in the shower as I entered the room. I staggered over and placed my gun in the corner. He came out with a strange look on his face. He said: "I'm so tired, I can hardly walk." "Oh, you'll get used to it," I responded, "We're all just a little out of shape." That night at dinner, the outfitter, at his private table, yelled out questions from different guides about all of the activities. It appeared I was the only one who had seen an elk. Had I known this, I would have shot that spike and auctioned it off. Or, perhaps we could have a lottery and the last hunter standing would get the spike.

The next morning, I was the first person in the dining room again. Most were late in getting up. A couple of the younger hunters bounced down the stairs, but the others sort of melted down the stairs. Some were unshaven, some had bloodshot eyes; it was a sight to behold. The food was great. We could order any kind of breakfast and there was plenty of it, but most didn't appear to be eating much. The outfitter barked out his orders for the day and before I knew it, we were on our way again. The other hunter had recovered by now and was optimistic about the day's hunt. Today, our guide said: "We were going to the *other* side of the mountain."

The second day was about the same. I had now convinced my guide to slow down and to rest more often. We walked all morning, but found no sign of any elk anywhere. We were working our way in a northeasterly direction and came upon a ridge. There was a well-marked trail. It showed heavy horse use. I stopped and looked. In spite of my hatred for horses, I almost wished that I had one to ride that trail.

I asked the guide what trail we were following. He didn't know. We decided to follow it north for a while. It was marked at regular intervals. It must have been an important trail. The guide was walking ahead of me. I stopped and read an inconspicuous sign. I yelled to my guide: "Hey, I know what trail this is! It's the Lewis and Clark Trail. This is the boundary between Idaho and Montana. We can legally hunt on the left side but the right side is Montana." I'll confess, that if an elk had shown itself in Montana, it would have been in serious trouble.

This new geographic information pumped me up for the rest of the day. I remembered much of the Lewis and Clark history and all that they had gone through on their 28-month journey with the "Core of Discovery" group of men. How could a guide know so little of the country that he was hunting? That reminded me of an Alaskan fishing trip where a native guide, that I was supposed to be using, had arrived, for the first time, three days before I did. We walked the trail for a couple of miles and turned to make a circle back to the suburban. I did see where a couple of elk had crossed from Idaho into Montana.

Our slower pace made this day of hunting easier. The guide had also reduced the distance traveled. My philosophy was: "If you are not going to see elk, it is better not to see elk in a shorter distance." Upon our return to the vehicle, we discovered that our companions had quit at noon today. The hunter was terribly discouraged. I couldn't blame him but failure was almost an old friend to me.

I was anxious to see how every one looked after the second day. Worse than the day before. Not a single hunter had seen an elk. I asked Mark how his day had gone. He said that he had spooked a rag horn bull on the bank of a road but did not have time for a shot. So, he and I were the only hunters to even have seen an elk. This was not good news. That night, at dinner, two hunters from Wisconsin told the outfitter that they were going to drive home in the morning. Four down and 15 to go.

I noticed that the loud and exciting noise at meal times was significantly reduced. However, when the guides would come into the dining room to eat, the outfitter bellowed in his same fashion from his private table in the corner. I began to think of him as "Captain Queeg," from the classic *Caine Mutiny* novel. I began to look for the palm tree in the corner.

Day three, little change. Everyone got up a little later and some hunters were not up when Mark and I left for our daily ordeal. I asked again, why we were hunting the same areas and where was the private, leased ground? The guide finally answered: "I go where I am told to hunt." This day, my knees were aching as we started out, not a good sign. I told my guide to plan a very short circle and that we could find a good viewpoint and spend more time watching. Our companion guide and hunter had followed a similar plan. We met that night and there was a gloom of disappointment that could have been cut with a knife.

When we returned to the base of our operations, I found that two other hunters were in downtown Wisdom and were planning on leaving that night. Six down and 13 to go. Mark appeared to be in better spirits, bless his heart. I felt guilty for having been responsible for his ordeal, even though I was paying for the trip. I told him that I was not going to hunt in the morning. I was going to drive four hours northeast and visit my brother who lived in Columbia Falls, Montana. Mark responded that he would find an elk, if there was one in that area of the state. He must have inherited some of my weakness for persistence.

I left at 4:00 a.m.; everyone else in the building was asleep. I had been warned to watch for deer along the highway since that area was heavily populated with them. As I drove through the darkness toward Columbia Falls, I had to be very alert. The deer were everywhere. I have never driven a hundred miles, through a canyon, with so many deer.

I reviewed our hunting situation. I knew now that the guides were moving the different hunters around the same areas from day to day, and apparently this would go on until the hunt was over. There were no private land leases. None of the hunters except Mark and I had seen an elk. Not a shot had been fired. There were no repeat clients. Several of the hunters were leaving early. I was caught in **The Idaho Scam!**

That outfitter had a cash-producing, legal operation, at $2000/hunter. Some hunters were only staying a couple of days. No animals had to be caped or processed. No trucks, 4-wheelers, or pack animals were needed. The overhead and effort were minimal and so the profits were high.

I spent a few hours with my brother, Ray, in Columbia Falls and then drove back to Wisdom. I met Mark as he came in from hunting. He had an agonizing look on his face. He said his feet and knees were killing him and that they had not seen any elk. I reviewed my analysis of the operation with him. I apologized for getting him involved. I told him it was almost as bad as floating the Kanectoc River! We agreed to leave in the morning.

We were a little late for breakfast the next morning. I couldn't figure out how many of the original 19 were still there. At least four were going out to hunt on the last day. The outfitter did not appear for breakfast. His private table looked empty without him. However, another group would be coming in on Sunday night and I was confident he would be sitting there by then. Mark and I just quietly packed our gear and painfully worked our way down the stairs.

We arrived in Kamiah that evening and stayed at the same motel. We visited with Bill a little in the evening and then said goodbye to him in the morning. He was not surprised that we didn't get our elk. "I could have taken you hunting right around here," he reminded me. I said goodbye to Mark as he headed for Reno. I shook hands with Bill, and thanked him again for the gun.

Bill called me in May of the next year. We talked, but I couldn't figure out exactly what he wanted. He finally said: "I just wanted to hear a few kind words." Hopefully, I gave him some. He died the next day.

The Realtor

In my opinion, the most dishonest people in business are guides and outfitters. Now second place is another matter. I am undecided if it is used car salesmen or realtors. A recent experience reinforced my confusion.

I sort of retired from work in 1996. I came to Utah and purchased some property. I met a realtor named Treavor Gott. He treated me well in my real estate dealings. Later on, he approached me and offered me an opportunity to buy a share in a corporation that had a large piece of land in a prime area within the Ashley National Forest. I immediately became interested.

One spring evening in May, he took Barbara and me up to the property. I couldn't believe what I was seeing. There were elk everywhere, even walking down the road and in several draws and ridges. The deer were grazing here and there all along the way. The share offered hunting rights on the property, *if a permit could be acquired.* But then Treavor told me the public land was the west boundary and open for general hunting. "*You can have the best of both worlds,*" he said. I'll go with you if you want to hunt over there," he continued.

Anyone with the name of Treavor should have been a warning to me. I should have known that all of the elk that we saw would be the spring migration and most would be distributed over thousands of square miles of public land by the time hunting season arrived. I also found, later, that

203

the area was summer range for deer and most would have migrated down by the time the fall deer season arrived.

I bought a share in the property. One privilege of ownership was a site to build a cabin or use a travel trailer. I purchased a large, special made trailer in Kansas and pulled it to Utah. It was too large for general use but would be perfect until I could build the cabin that I planned.

It was too late to get a special permit for our private land or any other private land in the area. But since I had the best of both worlds, I was not concerned. As elk season approached, I scouted and explored vast areas of land, both our land and the public land. The night before the season, I drove my 4-wheeler on a trail to decide where to begin the hunt the next morning. I spooked a small herd of elk and that helped me make my decision.

I was staying on the mountain by myself. Although this is lonesome, I have always considered myself pretty good company, and, often, the loneliness and isolation from others becomes a challenge and attraction, in itself. The elk season on the open area lasted 10 days. The opening day was beautiful. I arose, had my breakfast and was ready. My 4-wheeler was packed the night before. By daylight, I was silently moving up a long draw that had intermittent water, one of the few places on that side of the mountain.

About 8:00, I heard a bull bugle. I had been listening in the evenings and sometimes I could hear several from all sides of the private property. Often, on the private property, I could see the elk moving up the sides of the ridges. I had just purchased a new type bull bugle and had practiced it, with limited success. I waited a few seconds and answered.

In about 30 seconds, the bull answered me. I was excited. I knew that I could eventually work my way to that bull. It sounded as if it was coming from down the ridge. It bugled again. I moved faster toward the sound. I answered again. Sure enough, we were having some kind of a bull elk conversation.

I had been reading a few days earlier, not to bugle more often than necessary. Bulls often may become intimidated and move their cows away from a bull moving in. Other hunters think that this will make the bull anxious and ready to fight for the cows. I gave one more call which was immediately answered. I was getting very close. The sound was loud, distinct and had a tone of frantic appeal. I didn't make any more calls as I worked my way down the canyon.

The last call I heard appeared to be right in front of me in a small stand of Ponderosa Pine. I crouched down. That bull must be right there. Then I saw him…a hunter in full camouflage, right in front of me about 30 yards away. I was angry, disappointed and embarrassed to think that I could be called in so easy! I walked up to the hunter, whom I was to learn later was from a prominent family in the valley, and said: "Where's your orange clothing?" "I don't have it on," he replied. "I can see that," I responded. "Do you know the law?" He didn't respond. In Utah it is required that a hunter have 400 square inches of orange, in addition to an orange hat. Bow hunters do not have to wear orange. I introduced myself to him and asked his name. I told him that I would be hunting in the area for the next few days and that the next time we met he had better be dressed in orange.

After this encounter, I continued down that ridge, up the next and made a long circle back to my 4-wheeler. By this time, it was mid-afternoon and I was very tired. I had lunch, rested and decided that I would watch a spring that evening since I didn't have the energy to walk any more that day. I was working my way to the spring when I met the elk caller again. He had on an orange hat but not the required 400 inches. I nodded to him as I drove past. I saw nothing as I hunted at the spring that evening.

I hunted for nine days that fall. My son, Clark, came for two days and we hunted together but during all of this time I saw nothing. The elk were in the general area but we could not locate them. Clark left the 8th day and I had one more day to hunt. Barbara was always concerned about me hunting alone. I was always cautious. I carried a cell phone. A repeater was located about three miles south so we had good reception from most hunting areas.

It snowed intermittently the last couple of days. One day, I returned to my travel trailer and noticed that a small herd of elk had passed within a few yards going up a nearby ridge. This was on private land, my land, but

I could not hunt there. The last afternoon, the snow was about 8 inches deep. I was on my 4-wheeler and decided that I would make a large circle around the major ridge on the private land. As I was about to return, I saw a herd of elk, in the middle of a pasture about 300 yards away. I revved up my machine and sped towards the elk. There were 26 head of cows and calves and two bulls. I watched them as they spooked and finally returned back to the ridge from which they came.

I could have easily shot at either bull, but I had to hunt the open, public area on the west. I thought that I would try one more evening over there. I went to the trailer, had a bowl of soup, warmed up and returned to my blind at the spring. Nothing came in that night, as usual. It was almost dark when I returned. It was cold and there was not another person anywhere in the area. I was chilled to the bone, but I made a promise to myself that night that I would get a bull the next year!

Treavor, of course, never hunted with me on public land. It was later before I found out that there were elk deprivation permits available to the shareholders and that I could have had one that year. Instead, he acquired them, gave them to his friends and used them himself.

The deer season opened on the private land and the open area two days after the elk season closed. Most of the snow had melted on the bottom of the draws. There were still a lot of domestic cows grazing on the property, for this was one motivation two other shareholders had for investing.

I had been watching the deer closely for several days. There were a few left, but not near the numbers found earlier in the year. When cold and snow comes, they leave, almost overnight for lower elevations. I had noticed for several mornings, a few deer would descend to the creek for water and then move off the private land to the public land on the west. I watched their route. My plan was to be on the first ridge west and intersect them *after* they left the private land and got on that best of both world's area.

The opening morning dawned clear and bright. I took my 4-wheeler and worked my way to the appointed ridge. The sun rose. I was beginning to glass the lower area intently, when I noticed cars and trucks coming from the south and entering the private land. I soon counted five vehicles between me and the proposed deer trail. It seemed that one of the shareholders decided to move his cattle off the mountain on the opening day of the season.

I was thoroughly disgusted and angry. I drove back to my campsite, loaded up everything, hooked on to the trailer and returned to Vernal. Next year would be different, I vowed. I also began to wonder about the character of my fellow shareholders.

Shared Shelter

I soon found myself elected President of the Corporation. I was unsuccessful in our Corporation draw for the two deer and one elk permits that were allocated. But I bought one elk permit at a very high but below market price (I hesitate to give the price since Barbara may read this book) and also acquired a deer permit. I also distributed the elk deprivation permits equally to the other shareholders.

I spent a lot of time during the summer of 1997 on the mountain. I and some hired high school students cleaned and cleared an old homestead and some abandoned sheep pens. We also removed some old and dangerous barbed wire fences. I loved every minute of it. We often saw elk and deer during our trips up and down the mountain.

Clark had drawn an elk permit. The special private land elk season lasted for about a month and started about a month before the open area season, on the west. I had hunted a couple of days without success before Clark came to join me. I enjoy hunting with my sons, although we don't always agree on everything.

Clark had never hunted elk before. I told him he must be fast and ready to shoot at all times. In hunting, every decision that can be made in advance, should be made, eliminating confusion. We started up a long ridge to the west of the private land. The private land was in the valley and all of the ridges, with the exception of one in the middle of the property was on BLM or Ashley National Forest land. Access, of course, was the great advantage and the opportunity to hunt the private land if desired.

We laboriously worked our way up the long ridge. We spooked several cows in an open meadow. They moved north and entered the deep timber of that ridge. We followed them and carefully watched at the edge of the timber. I saw a cow, Clark saw it also, but was too slow in deciding if he wanted to shoot or not. He was disappointed as we continued to the top of the ridge and then made a long circle back to the valley. We returned to our 4-wheelers and drove back to our campsite for lunch.

I was exhausted. Clark was tired, but I was twice his age. He sat and rested and I went to bed. I rested but didn't sleep well. I arose in mid-afternoon and we decided that we would go back and hunt where we had been in the morning. A cow had been coming in on a spring and Clark wanted to hide in an old barn and wait for it. I wanted to go back to the high ridge where we saw the elk in the morning. Treavor Gott was at his cabin and mentioned that he might go with us.

The weather had been threatening all day, with heavy clouds coming and going. Occasionally a few drops would fall but nothing of significance. When we left that afternoon, heavy clouds were gathering in the west. We arrived at Treavor's cabin. He said that he would hunt low, I would hunt high and Clark would watch the spring.

That afternoon, I would not walk up the ridge, but would take my machine as far as possible and then stalk from there. I slowly worked my way up the ridge. The views from that ridge west, were awesome. I would stop and rest and watch for elk and deer sign. I saw nothing.

I parked my 4-wheeler several hundred yards below the saddle on the ridge. It was becoming increasingly cloudy. I found a place to stop and glass the area. I hid behind some cedar trees. I stayed there for about an hour and then became chilled. Walking would warm me up so I thought that I would go to the saddle, cross the boulder pile, and check the other side of this huge mountain.

As I scrambled over the rocks, rain began to fall, lightly at first but then more intensely. Thunder bellowed across the valley and lightning flashed on the higher peaks to the north. I continued my climb. By the time I reached the saddle, rain was pelting me from the west. On the saddle were several very large spruce trees, with spreading branches a few feet from the ground.

Three of these trees made a triangle of protection. Hiding under large trees on a ridge in a lightning storm was not very smart, I thought, but I didn't want to get any wetter than necessary. Standing under a Spruce tree is good for about ten minutes of heavy rain. After that, the water comes pouring down and it can be worse than standing out in the open, with the exception of the wind. I stamped my feet and looked at my watch. It had been raining for about 15 minutes, with continuous thunder and lightning to the north as the storm came in from the High Uintah Mountains.

I had on a rain jacket but not rain pants. My feet and Levis below the knees were now soaked and the wetness was moving up my legs. I moved into the triangle of trees deeper, but that didn't help. Then, all of a sudden, from the east, right in front of me, charged a cow elk. She was within six feet of me before she saw me. Her eyes grew large; she reared back to prevent hitting me. Her calf, close behind, bounced off her rear quarters. In a second, she snorted, whirled and was gone into the rain, her calf closely behind. I thought: "Wow, **shared shelter!**"

The rainwater was now running off every branch of all of the trees. The wind continued and so did the thunder and lightning. It was now almost 7:00 p.m. and getting darker. I had to make a decision. Should I wait for the rain to stop or should I "bite the bullet" and start down across those slick boulders?

I moved out from the trees. Something caught my eye below on a trail that came up from deep timber. Elk! Here they came and I started counting them. Thirteen cows and calves. Not a spike or a bull. The wind was whipping in all directions. They were 30 feet away. The lead cow caught my scent and immediately bolted and was gone. The others followed her over the saddle. I had a cow permit and so did Clark. But this was no time to be shooting cows. That could come later in the fall. Cows are easy to get, or so I thought.

As these thoughts passed through my mind, movement down the same trail caught my eye. I moved back slightly in the trees. Elk! This was an exact replay of a few minutes before. I counted them as they gathered right in front of me. Eleven cows and calves. No spike or bull. As they hesitated, several must have caught my scent and they were gone, exactly the same as the first group.

Twenty-four cows and calves but not a spike or bull. Why were they moving so fast in a rainstorm? I always thought that elk holed up during a storm. However, the thunder had been intense for several minutes.

By now the light was beginning to fade but the rain was not so intense. I still had to make the decision of when to start down that boulder strewn trail. For the past several minutes, I kept checking my scope. It was fogging from the rain and the difference in temperature between the metal and the air. The rag that I was using was now soaked.

I had decided to start down and was putting on my backpack when I saw a movement down the same trail. I dropped the backpack and stepped back into the trees. Here came the herd bull, slowly and without concern for where all of his cows had disappeared. I first saw him at 125 yards. I threw up my scope. All fogged over. I quickly grabbed my rag and wiped it. It was much clearer now. When shall I shoot? How soon will it get my scent from the whirling wind that still persisted? Shall I try a frontal shot in the chest as he walked? I might hit the head and ruin the antlers. None of my philosophy of making decisions in advance seemed to apply!

He kept plodding up the trail, moving his head up and down and twisting it from side to side in a strange manner. He was now at 60 yards and I knew he would catch my scent. Suddenly he stopped and looked right at me, but I didn't move. He moved slightly to his left as if making a turn. This gave me a partial broadside shot. I squeezed the trigger. I could actually see the bullet hole in his wet side. It made a red ring about 3 inches in diameter. He turned slightly and acted as if he was going to bound back down the trail. I slammed the second shot into him and it hit about 4 inches from the first shot. The second shot got his attention. He moved slightly to the left and collapsed, his feet going out from under him.

I was so excited that I was shaking. I paced the distance as I approached him. I did not want to ruin the front of him so I did not bleed him in the normal way. I needed a large cape, below his front shoulders for mounting. I looked at him. A huge animal with a heavy 5 x 5 rack, not the usual raghorn bull found on the mountain. I looked at his ivory front teeth. They were worn and slightly colored. These teeth were called "ivories" and the larger, more colored ones were a great trophy to elk hunters.

My lower back had been tender and sore for days and now it was hurting worse as I tried to bend over and field dress him. I finally got into a prone position to finish the job. It was now dark. The rain had stopped but the wind was still blowing and I was chilled to the bone. The elk would be fine. Tomorrow, we would have to quarter him and carry him across the boulders and down to our 4-wheelers. The trail was too rough to get the machines on the saddle.

I painfully arose and retrieved my knife, bone saw and backpack. I found my flashlight and slowly started down the hill in the dark. I couldn't remember exactly where I parked my 4-wheeler. I got across the boulders and then on into the timber. However, at this point, there were two trails down and I selected the wrong one. I soon realized that I was below the machine. I went back up and took the other trail and soon found it. By now, I was very cold. As I warmed up the machine and started down the hill, I realized this was my most exciting elk hunt!

Left, the 5 x 5 bull elk killed in the rain storm. Right, Clark hanging quarters to cool, Utah, 1997.

I finally reached the bottom of the ridge. I knew that Clark would have returned home and that Trevor would be safely in his cabin. As I started down the trail in a south western direction, I came to the intersection going to Trevor's cabin. I wanted to share my story with him. However, I found him and his wife too preoccupied with their evening's activities. They were more concerned with my muddy boots tracking up their carpet than my elk hunting success. However, Treavor said that he would help me pack the elk out in the morning.

I returned to our campsite. Clark was there, waiting and very concerned about my late arrival. It makes most people nervous when they realize an old man is hunting on the mountain and has not returned before dark. I told the whole story and he was pleased. He told me that he had missed a cow several times. He had to use one of my extra guns since some screws on his gun had vibrated loose from being carried on the 4-wheeler. He was not used to the scope and the different action.

The next day we picked up Treavor and returned to the saddle on that ridge. The elk looked larger in the daylight. This was the biggest bull that had been killed in recent years. However, it was certainly not a record in any sense of the word, but it was a worthy trophy, having been earned from days and days of hunting over a two-year period. We quartered him and packed out the head and two quarters. Later in the day Clark and I finished carrying out the last two quarters. Treavor did not return to help.

In a few weeks the deer season opened. I had seen several very large buck deer. One came near my travel trailer one morning. One day I saw six worthy bucks in one herd. On opening day I saw one small four point and a spike. I let both go by. I continued to hunt the whole general area without success. The deer appeared to almost *always* migrate out before the season opened. I also hunted in the best of all world's area without success.

I failed to get my travel trailer out before the snows came. It remained on the mountain all winter. I took it out the following May. It was none the worse for having been there, except some rub marks left from a few itching steers wandering the area.

The Gun Rest

In the late fall of 1997, after having had several negative experiences with other shareholders, I decided to give up my share in the corporation. As President, I saw the underbelly of that organization. I did not like what I saw: stealing timber, possible poaching, unpaid grazing fees, misappropriation of funds, etc. I decided that I did not want to be involved any longer. I remembered the adage: "If something appears too good to be true, it probably is." Although I lost a lot of money, not examining my contract closely, I had some valuable experiences.

However, I still had a deprivation cow permit. I started hunting cows soon after the bull season closed. However, by then the weather had warmed and the elk were really spooky. After the first significant snow, a friend and I jumped several cows one afternoon but I missed at 350 yards. My accuracy was not very good at those distances. This friend, Ed Souders, promised to help me later in the year.

It was the Wednesday before Thanksgiving. I was bored and wanted to go up and hunt elk. Ed was in Colorado for the holiday. I didn't bother to tell Barbara where I was going. I loaded up one of my 4-wheelers, took what I thought I would need, including my cell phone, and headed up the mountain. I arrived at 2:00. It was clear when I left home but by now it was very cloudy and threatening.

I unloaded my machine, put a shovel and my gun on the front gun rack and headed out. I passed over the north saddle of the ridge, watching for elk. I headed to where we had missed the cows a few weeks before. As I traveled the familiar, pleasant, but rough trail east, I thought how I loved this property and how I would truly miss it. I had explored all parts of it. I knew areas that other shareholders had never seen. I had found timbered draws, secret trails and secretly built tree stands, apparently built by poaching-prone shareholders.

But my mind came back to the present, Where to hunt today? I might try to get up the east ridge but the snow was probably too deep and I did not have chains on my machine. I kept following the trail as it meandered northward. Suddenly, I turned off. I would hunt a large box canyon on the north of the property. I had never seen an elk in there but it was sheltered. As I continued, I had to cross a running spring and a deep bog. But my 4-wheeler had no problem with those minor obstacles.

I continued through some scattered Quaky groves. I looked for sign as I moved along. Suddenly I saw where elk had passed through that area recently, at least in the last day or two. I turned the machine west and started following them. I glanced up to the end of the canyon and there, half way up a ridge, I saw them. Several elk moving east. I had spooked them and they were moving away. I stopped and quickly slipped off my 4-wheeler.

I tried to get my gun off the rack. It was secured by rubber straps. However, the weather had cooled since I put the gun on and they were frozen and shrunk. I pulled and pulled and finally ripped the gun off and pumped a shell in the barrel. The group of elk had split. Three had run to the left and disappeared into the trees. The other three had turned broadside as they continued across the ridge. They were now about 275 yards, a fairly long shot. I pulled up my gun, moved the scope to 6 power and looked. There was a young bull, and two cows without calves. One cow was darker than the other and looked larger than the bull.

That cow would be the best eating and the one to shoot. I looked again. It had stopped and was watching me. I started to shoot and realized that

I was nervous and would not hit it, off-hand, at that distance. I needed a rest, but there was nothing around. Then suddenly I realized I could use my 4-wheeler as a **gun rest.** I dropped to the snow covered ground. A little low but usable. By now the elk were moving again, and the shot would be further. I placed the cross hairs behind the shoulder and squeezed off a shot. Nothing happened. The three elk moved further away. Suddenly, the three in the timber started my way. Now what? I scoped the three as they came out of the timber. I then put my scope back on that large, dark brown cow. I looked and suddenly it just toppled over! I knew it was dead.

In the meanwhile the other three were coming directly at me. They acted as if they didn't see me. There were two cows and a spike. They were strung out by now and each swerved when it got close enough to realize I was standing there. I had finally bagged my cow. I drove my machine over to the beginning of the ridge. As I got off, I realized, from the sign that they had been staying here in this small protected area for several days. The spring originated out of the ridge and gently flowed southward through the meadow. The elk had everything they needed right there until I had invaded their privacy.

I walked up and looked at the cow. She was very large, as big as a young bull, fat and in great shape. She would make prime eating. I cut her throat to enhance the bleeding. I looked down and realized it was steeper and further than I thought to the bottom. I looked west; no chance to come in from that direction. I looked east and that direction didn't look any more promising. Suddenly, I felt worried. How was I going to get that cow out by myself?

I didn't field dress her. I knew if I had problems pulling her, having her field dressed could make it more difficult. I went back down and put my Suzuki in low range, 4 x 4, posi-traction. This is the only machine on the market with such options. The snow was not deep on the south side, but I only managed to go a few yards until the slope was so steep that I was beginning to teeter backwards. Teetering backwards is not a pleasant feeling. I slowly backed down. I got off and looked at the distance to the bottom of the ridge. If I could pull her half way down, perhaps, I would have enough chains, straps, cables, etc. to hook her on to my pickup and get her down the hill.

My pickup was on the other side of the ridge, three miles away. Time was wasting. I climbed on and headed toward the pickup as fast as I could, working around all of the barriers. When I got to the trail, I could move very rapidly, using my old tracks to guide me. I quickly put my ramp down when I arrived and pulled the snow laden machine into the pickup bed. I then headed around the ridge to the elk from the south.

I noticed that it was starting to snow as I pulled off the road and worked my way toward the elk. I could not use the same route. It was much too rough for a truck. Instead I worked my way eastward to the edge of a ridge running north and south and then worked my way north along an old cattle trail. I was doing fine until I came to a bog. Bogs are very dangerous for trucks, not so for 4-wheelers. Trucks will bog down from their weight, where the 4-wheelers plow right across.

I walked back and forth across, trying to determine how soft it was. I didn't have much choice. I sighed as I pulled up, accelerated hard and ploughed through the bog. I made it through. I looked back at the tracks and they were very deep. I might have to find another crossing on the way back.

I climbed the ridge and reached the cow. She was starting to get stiff and difficult to turn over. I started pulling her down the hill. I did well for 50 yards but then she got caught in some brush. I walked down the hill to the pickup. If I could remove a tree, I could back to the base of the ridge. I removed the dead tree and slowly backed the truck as far as possible. I paced the distance to the elk.

I took out chains, straps and everything that I had and tied them all together. I put the strap around the cow's neck and laid out all of the rest of the line toward the truck. I pulled tight. I had about four inches to spare. I tied the end chain on to the bumper. I got in, revved the Dodge diesel pickup up and took off. I looked in the rear view mirror...elk, brush, trees and anything in the way was crashing down that hill.

I retrieved all of my line and prepared to field dress the animal. Then I remembered that Barbara didn't know where I was. I called her. She answered and said: "Where are you?" I proudly said: "On the mountain. I just killed a cow elk." "What are you doing up there this time of night? Who is helping you?" she asked. I paused a minute and said: "I don't need any help, I should be home by 8:00 p.m." Sometimes women worry needlessly.

I had another problem. My back had not healed from the bull elk hunt and it was more painful now. I could hardly bend over. I had a meat saw to help quarter the elk but I couldn't bend over for any length of time. Then I remembered, Bob Lucas and I used to use an axe. I quickly found one and in an hour the elk was dressed and quartered. By now it was dark and it was snowing harder. I remembered that I had not put my machine in the truck. If I put my machine in, where will I put the elk quarters and how will I lift them up? Ordinarily, I could easily lift an elk quarter, but not tonight.

The cow elk that had to be packed on the tail gate in the snow storm, Utah, 1997.

I always like outdoor challenges, but I didn't have anyone to discuss my ideas with out here alone. I put my ramp down and drove the machine on. If I was careful, I *might* be able to put all four quarters on the tailgate and tie them down with a chain. I took each quarter and pushed it up the ramp on my hands and knees. In another 30 minutes, I was loaded and ready to go. The truck was drooping a little in the back but a little weight never hurts when driving in the snow.

I carefully worked my way out. By now it was snowing so hard that I could not see my old tracks. I worked my way in the general southerly direction. I came across the creek again, lower down the meadow. I got out and checked it out. No bog. Solid bottom. I had it made. I returned home a little later than I thought. It was now 9:00 p.m. I walked in the house. I recognized from long experience, the look on Barbara's face. "When's supper?" I asked. I ate alone that night.

The Delta Force

I had hunted antelope in 1993, with Robert Rudde, or "Fat Bob," as I usually referred to him. I haven't written that experience yet. Every time I start to record it, the pain becomes awesome and I cry and then my vision is blurred. However, that didn't dampened my general interest in hunting antelope.

Some antelope hunting exists in Utah, but trying to get a permit is difficult. Utah's game and fish regulations are convoluted and unreasonable, the worst of any state where I have hunted. This is reflected in the scarcity of game and the frustration of sportsmen.

Wyoming is a little better. I talked a friend, Clark Hatch, into trying to draw an antelope permit in an area where I had hunted in the early 1950's. I told him of some of those early experiences and he was impressed enough to send in a deposit with me, on the buddy system, i.e., we would both get a permit or neither of us would get a permit. This system makes hunters true buddies.

I had not tried for a limited entry permit for many years. I thought that antelope were on an open license system, even for non-residents. I sent for the maps and regulations. I was amazed at all of the new areas, the complex rules for harvesting and the few permits allowed for large areas. There was no information in the orders about the success ratio for applicants.

I called the 800 number and asked for information. I talked to a very kind and helpful employee. He said: "I am on the computer and can give you any statistic that you want." I gave him three familiar looking areas. The success statistics ranged from 20:1 to 34:1. I was distressed and apparently communicated this to my G&F clerk. He then informed me that, for an additional $100, we could be placed in a "more successful pool of applicants."

I then asked what those statistics were. These ranged from 3:1 to 7:1. I chose the 3:1 area. That's not too bad, but then I remembered I had never won anything in my life. We each, choked a little, and submitted our $275. I then remembered when I could hunt antelope for $5 and could hunt in any number of different areas. Fortunately, I did not think about that *before* I wrote the check.

In July, we received our permits. In the meanwhile, Clark had taken a summer position as a campground host at Devil's Tower National Monument, in northeastern Wyoming. We would have to coordinate our schedules well. The season opened on September 15. Clark had just purchased a nice, new travel trailer and he would bring it down for us to use. Now that's my kind of buddy.

Our hunt area was on the south side of Highway #220, from Alcova clear to Muddy Gap Junction. I knew this area well. It was near the Rattlesnake Mountains, The Sun Ranch and Horse Creek and all of those other memorable places of past hunting and fishing ordeals.

We met at Alcova at noon the day before the season was to open. He brought his travel trailer and I brought two 4-wheelers. I wanted to see if they would be useful for hunting. In the 1940's and 1950's, they didn't exist. Much of this area was windblown sand and some kind of 4 x 4 was needed. I was driving my Dodge Ram 2500 4 x 4 diesel Pickup. We appeared to be well equipped.

We camped at the Pathfinder Dam Campground. This was a pleasant area near the old hand built granite dam. Using a travel trailer is a delight, compared to the old tent camping. We were set up in a few minutes and

I put some dinner in the Dutch oven. And I proceeded to give Clark a tour of the area. My Great Grandfather was a teamster and he freighted supplies to the workers while they completed the dam from 1900–1907. The North Platte River now has four major reservoirs along this area. Pathfinder was the first constructed and my favorite reservoir.

Later in the afternoon we scouted to see where we wanted to hunt in the morning. I had maps showing private vs. public land. I remembered an old ranch south of the highway about 20 miles. But we soon found the Pathfinder Land and Cattle Company had purchased the old ranch and many other isolated sections of land in the area. This had become a huge ranch. We drove to the ranch headquarters to ask permission to hunt. We were told the wealthy owner lived in St. Louis, Missouri and ranching was one of his hobbies. This meant that he could manage it and not have to worry about it being profitable, as had all of the previous owners.

We noticed a new chapel had been built at the headquarters. The owner was a Catholic and had built this chapel for his own use. Apparently, at times, he brought out a priest with him to visit the ranch. So goes modern ranching.

We noticed several huge buck antelope grazing around the chapel and outbuildings at the headquarters. I asked Clark: "Do you think it would be sacrilegious to shoot one of bucks so close to that chapel?" He responded: "Heck, no, I'm not Catholic, I'm Mormon."

We finally found someone on the ranch who could give us permission to hunt the following day. We found a ranch hand's wife, who visited with us. She told us she and her husband had owned the ranch until the mid-1980's when cattle ranching became so difficult. They had lost the ranch to the bank and then hired on as workers with the new owner.

She gave us some general directions where the private land would be. However, later, we found the private land well marked by attractive, expensive signs. I knew that we would be hunting on both private and public land. But now, I felt better for having received permission. I also promised the woman we would give her the $15 Landowner rebate forms for submitting to the G&F Department. She appeared as if she could use the money.

Before I left, I inquired if the wife had seen any game wardens in the area. I could get some information from them about general hunting conditions, movement of antelope, etc. She said that they had a new warden assigned to area and, "she was a woman." The wife went on about "how difficult the new female warden had been when discussing game issues." This sounded interesting to me. I had never met a female warden. In past years I had taught many wildlife majors, but none of the women that I knew had become wardens. I had a feeling I might meet her on this trip.

The next morning dawned bright and beautiful and *no wind.* Having lived in Wyoming for so long, thanks are always given for any day when the wind does not blow. In fact, the wind blows so hard in some parts of Wyoming that residents use a log chain for a wind sock. Concern is seldom shown until the chain is blowing straight out from the post.

We decided that we would work our way south toward the old former ranch where I used to hunt. Shortly after light, we spotted a small buck running across the road. It stopped at about a 100 yards. Clark scoped it but we decided that it was too small and it was too early in the hunt to take him. We continued on for several miles and only saw a few does. I couldn't believe the shortage of animals.

We saw a few does before we drove down the long hill to the old ranch house. It looked different than I had remembered. Had something been done to it during the past 40 years? Probably not, as we grow older, our mental hard drives often get emotional spots on them.

The ranch looked abandoned, however, on the far side of the barn, two ranch hands were trying to load a piece of a tractor on a pickup. I walked over and introduced myself to them. They were not very interested in visiting, but I insisted, by saying: "Where are all of the antelope? I used to hunt around here 50 years ago." This 50 years statement caught their attention. One, stopped, looked closely at my wrinkles and missing hair.

"There's not many around any more. We haven't seen many lately at all. You should drive west and work your way over in that direction," the older man said. I then asked: "When was the *last time you saw an antelope?*" The smaller man interrupted by saying: "There was a herd on the other side of that barn, north about a mile, last night." That was good enough for me and Clark and I headed in that direction.

We drove to the barn. We saw the herd, with one large buck at the end. I parked the pickup between the barn and the antelope. We watched the antelope begin to run up the hill and over a ridge. I said: "Clark, this is a good time to try out our 4-wheelers." We unloaded them, packed a few things and started toward where the antelope disappeared.

I suggested to Clark that he go west, since they were heading in that direction. I would go east, in case they reversed directions. Normally, unless, shot at, antelope will go over a ridge or two and quiet down. This was not the case for this herd. I laboriously worked my way over five different ridges but never saw them. We met back at the barn. Clark said: "Did you hear me shoot?" "What were you shooting at?" I asked. "Two nice bucks came by but I missed them both," he answered. I hadn't seen a single animal and he had two come right by him.

I decided that there so few antelope in this large area that hunting by 4-wheeler was not practical. We unhitched the trailer and we began to work our way north and then west. We traveled the most difficult roads that paralleled the distant highway on the north. We worked our way south to the pine covered hills. There were no antelope around. We occasionally would see a few does, but no bucks. I couldn't believe that the Wyoming Game and Fish Department could have mis-managed that great resource. In the old days there would have been scores of animals in the area.

By noon, we had meandered about 20 miles west towards Muddy Gap Junction. Most of the land was public with an occasional section or two belonging to the Pathfinder Land and Cattle Company.

My memory went back to 40 years ago when I would hunt the area and when there were vast herds. How disappointed I was. By now we were entering an area with small hills and sand blown ridges, covered with a little grass and a lot of sagebrush. A great place for antelope. I told Clark that we should find antelope in this area. I had just made that statement when I looked southwest, across a long sandy draw, and there in the bottom of it was a buck watching us as we slowly moved into the area. I stopped the truck and we glassed him. An average buck, but with the scarcity of game, we decided to go after him.

I told Clark that I would work my way around a hill on the south. "While the buck watched the truck, I would approach him from the southeast," I suggested. Clark agreed. I told him to: "be ready, the antelope could come toward him or to the north if I spooked him."

I ran, then walked then slowly crept over a rise on the south of the small hill. That buck had turned and was looking directly at ME! I quickly dropped to a prone position and found a clump of sagebrush for a gun rest. A long shot, at least 300 yards. He was looking straight at me. I aimed for the middle of his chest. There was a white spot that made a good target. I was shaking slightly as I squeezed off the shot.

The buck moved to the left and then looked at me again. I could see blood forming on his right front side. I had shot too far to the left. I knew that he was mortally wounded but could run a long distance. I would wait and soon he would lie down. All of a sudden, boom and Clark had opened up on him with his 7 mm. The antelope was running north. He stopped and looked at me again. Another shot from Clark and he was down for good.

I quickly went around the hill to the pickup and we drove over to the buck. He was a nice, mature buck. Although, according to the philosophy of some sportsmen, especially in Africa, the game belongs to the hunter who draws first blood, I told Clark that he made a good shot and asked him if he wanted the buck. He said "yes," and was delighted to claim him. I took several photos of Clark and his first antelope.

We were deeply involved in dressing the animal when I heard a pickup behind me. I looked and there was a warden working his way over to our kill site. "Oh, good, now we can meet this female warden," I told Clark.

However, a man got out, hitched up his gun belt and greeted us. "I see you got an antelope," he said. I didn't know what he expected us to be hunting, but I said: "Yes, he's a nice buck." He wanted to see my license. I had to stop, clean my hands and show him everything.

After we were through, I asked him where all of the antelope were. "They are everywhere," he said. Why, " I just saw a few several miles west of here." I told him how it used to be, before his was born. He wasn't impressed. "We have educated wildlife biologists now and they know what they are doing. Why this area is one of our prime trophy areas." I persisted by saying, "If this is the case, where are all of the trophies?" We told him we had one more antelope to get. He didn't respond but gave us an informal salute and went back to his pickup.

Antelope have to be carefully dressed and cleaned, if the meat is to be edible. We dressed and skinned him, and wrapped him in a clean mesh covering. He would be prime eating…that is, if you like antelope. I enjoy antelope steak, fried crisp with fried potatoes.

We had forgotten to eat our lunch with all of the excitement. We grabbed our lunch and drinks and sat down on the shady side of the pickup. It was too warm to eat in the direct sun. Our enforcement friend had come from the west and that was the direction we wanted to go. We were in one of the finest habitat areas around and we had seen one buck and no does. This was not very promising.

We continued to work our way west. I had never been this far west and so was not sure where we were in relation to the Sun Ranch and the new Mormon Handcart Visitor Center. The road went through some more private land with a new house. I wanted to turn north and did so at the next gate. I did not see fresh tracks, so the warden must have come through on another road.

What had become a road was now more of a trail but it was not difficult to follow. We topped a rise and below was a grass lined draw running for a mile to the west. I slowed down. Off to the right, were several antelope. Two or three looked like bucks. I quickly got out of the truck. One buck was moving to the right and one was going away. They were not very spooky, but they did not like our looks.

I scoped them. They were all bucks, six in total, with two quite small. Clark was watching them intently. "Which one's the largest," I asked. "The one moving to the right," Clark responded. "That one on the ground is larger," I said. They were all getting very nervous and beginning to move to the right. The one on the ground appeared to think that we could not see him. I put the cross hairs slightly behind his shoulder and squeezed lightly. The buck never moved. The first time I had ever found a buck that continued to try to hide after seeing him.

This buck was a twin to the one shot earlier in the day. We prepared the carcass in the same careful way. We wanted all of the meat to be good. We continued to wind our way northwest until we came to a well traveled county road and it took us to the highway. We came out about a mile west of the Mormon Handcart Visitor Center. I determined that I shot the buck due south of that area about 3 miles.

We traveled east for several miles before we approached a Wyoming Game & Fish Department roadblock. They were intent on stopping everyone that looked like a hunter. This surprised me since we had only seen two or three hunting parties in hundreds of square miles of area. I pulled off into the designated "search area." I looked around. Four pickups, with people wandering around in every direction. Was this the **Delta Force?** Two men approached us with serious looks on their faces. I expected to see a black helicopter hovering above at any minute.

One man reviewed all of our licenses and checked our Pickup plates. The other began, what appeared to be, an autopsy of the antelope. I was ready to be "spread eagled," and "strip searched" at any moment. Then, I thought: "Where is that female warden?" When they finished. I said: "I hear a new female warden has been assigned this area. Is she here today?" One officer glanced at the other and had a strange smirk on his face. "She's driving that pickup over there," he said.

An average buck antelope, taken by the author, without the help of the Delta Force, Wyoming, 1999.

I looked and saw a cloud of dust from a truck going at breakneck speed along the fence line. The pickup was bouncing violently which meant there was no road there. "Where's she going, I asked?" "She thinks there might be a hunter over that ridge, he replied. I was glad I wasn't hunting over that ridge, I might have been "strip searched," after all.

Guilty as Charged

One bright, sunny day in February, 1998, a friend, Ed Souders called and said that he was bored and did I want to go for a ride up on the mountain and see some new country. Ed was an old timer around here and knew a lot of the country. I said: "You bet, I have an industrial strength case of boredom myself. I'll pick you up." I dropped by Blimpie's and got a couple of sandwiches and other junk food for the trip. Ed is the junk food king of the world.

We took my pickup and headed up over the mountain toward Flaming Gorge, on the Ashley National Forest. It was a bright day. The snow had melted from the highway as we sped along. We decided that we would look for elk and deer in some of the more hidden places. We found several herds as we went by the Phosphate Plant's private land and then several groups grazing on the south sides of the ridges.

We slowly crossed the dam and wound our way further up the mountain. After we got out on top, Ed began to show me several roads that I had never traveled. He took me to a couple of remote camp grounds and a launching ramp on the lake. Then we headed out towards the upper part of the lake. He told me to turn off on the Antelope Flats road and then we could work our way south and glass that ridge. There were often elk there he told me.

It was now about 11:00. The sun was high and bright and it was one of those winter days that warm men's souls. We were sitting on a little knoll, a mile or two off anything that could be called a road. Ed was now driving. We were having a soda and relaxing.

I noticed, coming from the east, a white pickup winding its way toward us, following our tracks off the road. It sped up as it approached us. It pulled around to the driver's side. I looked at the logo on the side and recognized it as one of the Utah Game and Fish Trucks, or to be formal Utah Department of Wildlife Resources.

A short man got out of the truck, adjusted his gun belt, as they all seem to do, and swaggered to the open window of our truck. "We've been watching you with our spotting scope, for quite some time," he informed us. Then he proceeded to tell us what roads we had been on and where we had stopped. "What are you hunting?" he questioned. I answered: "Nothing, there are no seasons open on anything."

"Do you have any long guns in the truck," he continued. "No, there isn't anything to hunt this time of the year." I responded. "Do you have any handguns in truck?" I was becoming agitated as I answered: "Yes, I have a handgun. I always carry a handgun in my truck." 'Let me see it," he ordered. I handed the gun to him.

"Is it loaded," he continued. "Yes, what good is a handgun, if it is not loaded. What am I supposed to do, use it as a club?" I answered. "Do you know the Utah state law about loaded handguns," he responded. "No, I am a new resident of the state." I replied. "You cannot have a shell in the barrel of a handgun. I am going to educate you," he hissed.

I didn't know exactly what he meant. "Educate me? I have been using and carrying handguns before you were born," I sharply responded. He pulled out his citation book and began to ask me all of the usual personal statistical questions. When he finished, he ripped out my copy and thrust it into my hand.

He climbed back into his pickup. He had a companion in the truck who had been watching the whole process. He worked his way out of the passenger's seat. He had long hair, a full beard and a Forest Service uniform on. He was obese. More of his stomach was hanging below his belt than was inside the belt.

He leaned into the window of our truck and belching, asked, "Do you know where you are?" I said: Yes, I am out in the wilderness on a beautiful day, minding my own business, being harassed by a couple of government bureaucrats." He then informed me that I needed a special permit because I had stopped on part of the Flaming Gorge National Recreation Area. He continued by telling me to get down below and buy a permit or he would give me a citation. He stumbled back and wormed his way up into the pickup.

To say they had ruined our day was to put it mildly. Where did they get the authority to behave in such a manner? Where was the due process procedure or reasonable cause? It's a wonder they didn't read me my Miranda rights. This was another example of government agencies out of control when dealing with the public.

I contacted the court before the deadline listed on the citation. The judge was a woman. I was relieved. Women are compassionate, I thought. The Judge asked: "How do you plead?" I answered, **"Guilty as charged."** But there are extenuating circumstances, I said. The Judge listened and then informed me that the normal penalty for this misdemeanor was a $185 fine and six months in jail. SIX MONTHS IN JAIL? For having a shell in the barrel of a handgun? The Judge said that she would inform me later of her decision. She later called me and fined me $110 and suspended the jail sentence.

The warden had educated me. I am still astounded at the whole experience. I began to question others of the law. Most had never heard of it. I then inquired about the regulations of a concealed handgun permit. I applied. I paid my fees, went to class, passed my shooting requirement and received the permit.

In my Pickup is the same gun, in the same place, with the same shell in the same barrel. *But I have been educated.* It is these types of experiences that try men's souls…and cause a strong lack of support and respect for our law enforcement agencies.

Re-Wind and Fast-Forward

The changes in technology and ease in living in my life have been astonishing. When I was a kid in a one-room school, we didn't even have ball point pens. Now, we are surrounded by cell phones, pagers, laptop and home computers, television and video recorders. The young people talk about *virtual reality* games. I am not interested in virtual reality. I want the *real experience and I want it first hand!*

I have tried playing some of the hunting games available on software for my computer. Although they are interesting, there is no personal involvement. Playing them does help pass the time away. One day, I was playing a deer hunting game. I looked out the window and the snow had stopped falling.

I shut off the computer, picked up my gun and went after the real animal! One of the problems with this generation may be in lacking a desire or a fear for *real involvement*.

Clark, a modern "Techie," who enjoys real involvement...especially with a good .30-06 dog, Kansas, 1991.

Computers frustrate me most of the time but they also fascinate me. Let's compare the human mind with a computer. The hard drive is similar to our memory. If you are seeking information from your hard drive or an auxiliary drive, you submit a word or series of words. And then you see what comes up! How many references did you get? Now, let's do the same thing into our personal memory. Put in a word like hunting or fishing. How many references did you get...perhaps many. Put in a word like blisters. Not so many references.

This book started with a desire to record a few of the more interesting stories for my family into an appendix to my condensed autobiography. But then I began putting in words and out came all of these stories and more...There are over 30 in this first book. Now, I have to work on the second book, either that or stop putting in words into my memory!

This morning, I awoke at 4:00 a.m., and foolishly put in several words and then waited for the results. Out came: **Quack-Quack; The Diving Dog; The Twin Bucks; The Confrontation; Extending the Season; Plenty of Antelope; Twenty-Five Straight; The Non-Resident Buck; The Social Antelope; The Worms are Gone: and I Wanna Go Home.** All of these new stories began to frustrate me. I can't get them all in this first book. I quickly locked my mental keyboard before I was flooded with more memories. You might be interested in these additional stories.

I hope that you have considered your time well spent if you have read this book. You have many interesting experiences of your own. Put in a few key words into your memory and see what comes out! Now, start to record them for your children and grandchildren.

The next two generations of hunters. Scott with his daughters, Kallie Jo, left, and Kiane, Kansas, 2000.

About the Author

Ben D. Mahaffey was born in a small oil town in Wyoming called Midwest, in 1932, to Roy Ray Mahaffey and Bertha Margaret Karman. He and his two brothers were orphaned in 1937. He was adopted by his father's brother, Dave Mahaffey, who is mentioned in the book.

He has received the following degrees: AA, Casper College, Wyoming; B.S., Colorado State University; M.S., Ph.D., Texas A&M University. He has consulted with, and taught, professionals from state and national resource management agencies. He is a journeyman printer and worked for newspapers in Wyoming and Colorado.

He is a veteran of the Korean War, serving as a medic in the Navy. He has worked for the U.S. Forest Service and taught at Texas A&M University and Kansas State University. He has been a private consultant to Fortune 500 Companies, and spent four years as a consultant for the U.S. Army, Pentagon.

For several years before retiring and moving to Utah, he was in private business. He has received regional and national honors for teaching and research. He has 25 publications in journals, magazines and books published during the 1960's-1980's.

He has been married to the former Barbara Alice Proud for 46 years. They are the parents of three sons, Mark, Reno, Nevada; Clark, Chandler, Arizona; and Scott, Randolph, Kansas. He has four grand-children. He resides in Vernal, Utah.